MW00768014

Like Father, Like Sons

Thom Hunter

Like Father, Like Sons

Fleming H. Revell Company
Old Tappan, New Jersey

Scripture quotation is from the King James Version of the Bible.
Quotation from SOME DAYS ARE DIAMONDS (SOME DAYS ARE STONE) by Dick Feller Copyright ©1975 Tree Publishing Co., Inc. International Copyright Secured. All rights reserved; used by permission of the Publisher.

Illustrated by Roselyn B. Danner.

Library of Congress Cataloging-in-Publication Data

Hunter, Thom.
Like father, like sons (and daughter, too).

1. Hunter, Thom. 2. Fathers—United States—Biography. I. Title.
HQ756.H86 1987 306.8'742 86-29819
ISBN 0-8007-1517-9

Published by the Fleming H. Revell Company
Old Tappan, New Jersey 07675
Printed in the United States of America

Dedication

TO sons, daughters, and fathers everywhere, but especially to Zachary, Russell, Donovan, Patrick, and Lauren, because fathers and their children need each other desperately. And finally and always, to Lisa, whom I loved long before I loved my children.

Preface

Parents are part future, part present, and part past. We are caught up in the present, worried about the future, and trying to learn from the past. And someone needs his diaper changed.

As a young husband, I had two very helpful and fulfilling opportunities. Before our first son was born, my wife and I spent one year as house parents in a private school in Texas. Our students were very wealthy—the kind of kids some would assume would have few cares in the world.

The very next year, with a baby in tow, we moved off to a ranch and became house parents for twelve high-school boys. For the most part, they were poor and troubled. In society's eyes they were the opposites of the private-school kids.

I discovered the difference between the groups was little or none. They were all kids. They hurt when afflicted. They misunderstood unless great pains were taken to make them understand. They rebelled when they felt threatened. They hid within themselves when they felt unsafe. They all had unmet needs.

Almost overnight it seems, we had four sons of our own and I was struggling to understand exactly what was expected of me as a father. Society, too, was struggling—trying to redefine the roles of mother and father in the face of equal rights and changing social values. I sensed a problem developing on a lower level: The children, those who would be most affected, had no idea what was going on all around them. Once again, we grown-ups were thinking it didn't matter that much; they'd understand it by and by.

I decided that fatherhood didn't need so much to be redefined as it needed to be rededicated; motherhood not so much redefined as remotivated. There had been too much emphasis on dividing and not enough on sharing. Both may make things equal, but sharing is a lot more rewarding.

Last, I grew tired of hearing about fathers being buffoons. We are so much more competent than people give us credit for. I also saw that some fathers, as long as no one thought they could do anything anyway, weren't going to do anything to change the image. Life is easier when people don't expect much of you.

This book covers almost two years in the life of my family, including the addition of our fourth son. And, after the book was completed, Lauren, our first daughter, fifth and last child, was born.

It is hoped that any reader who realizes how much space the telling of a few events in a father's life takes will realize there is a great deal to life as a parent. Whether you have sons or daughters, you have treasures.

I hope you find the stories humorous and touching. And I hope you realize I never believed fathers are buffoons. Fathers are just sons who grew up.

Contents

Like Father, Like Sons

1 The Daddy Diet

For the man who spends too much time at his desk and too little time exercising, who has begun to thicken around the middle and can't seem to shed pounds, there is an answer. It's called the Daddy Diet, or How to Lose Weight and Love It, and it works. I guarantee it. All a father has to do is attempt to do all the things for the children that his wife usually does during the hours he is safely at the office.

You may wonder how a few hours—or even a weekend, as was my case—spent baby-sitting ends up in a loss of pounds. The answer is simple. Like all successful diets, the Daddy Diet involves three things: more exercise, less food and adequate rest.

The exercise speaks for itself. After all, tossing one child up in the air (to the accompaniment of delighted shrieks) means you have to toss all three. You also get lots of exercise because while the diapers are stacked on the changing table, the diaper pins are upstairs, and the diaper pail is in the other bathroom. Where the kid is, is anybody's guess! However, tracking him down is half the fun of changing the diaper—the better half.

Exercise continues. After you get a super supper made, the littlest one into the high chair, the middlest one perched on the classified directory, and the oldest one shut up, you finally realize (after sitting down) that there are no drinks on the table. Up you go. See what I mean?

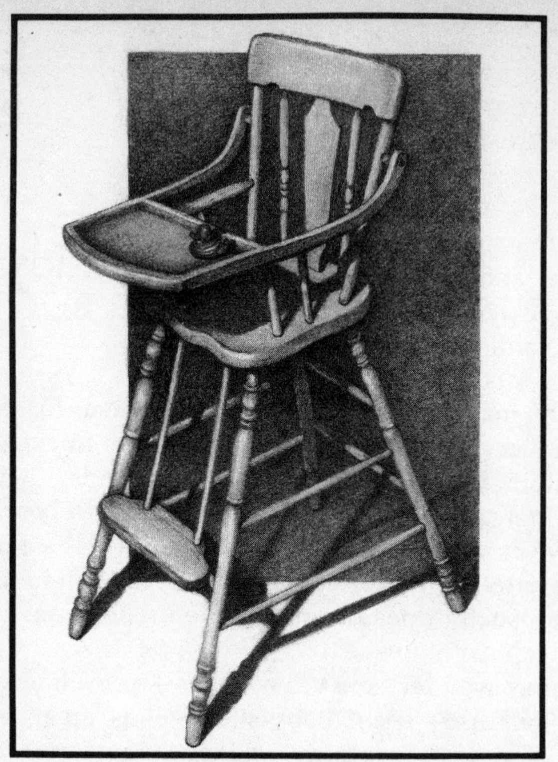

After you sit down again, the middlest one spills his juice on the tablecloth that your wife never leaves on the table when the kids are eating. You grab the sponge. The oldest refuses to drink what you fixed and wants water—something he has never wanted before. You get the water, which is easier than forcing him to drink juice. In the meantime, the littlest has fallen into silent slumber in his high chair and needs to be carried gently up to his bed, crusty though he is. Up again.

When you get back to the kitchen, you find the middlest has covered himself from head to toe because you forgot to slice the cherry tomatoes. Each whole tomato has exploded in his little mouth like a bomb, sending shell fragments all over. His meat untouched, but the bread and butter devoured off everyone's plate, including your own, he is no longer hungry and is climbing down, ready to leave his handprints throughout the house.

You decide it would be wiser to take him to the bathtub and let him soak, rather than wash the entire house later. Up you go again. Now you learn what it is like to undress a child who does not want to be undressed. Suddenly he has four arms and five legs and the strength of ten ordinary men. Finally in the tub, the water is pronounced too hot, then too cold. He glares at you from the shallow end of the tub and wants to know when Mommy is coming home.

The biggest, in the meantime, has decided to be helpful. He is making chocolate pudding. He has seen Mommy make it numerous times, and knows how easy it is to combine the ingredients and mix it up. When you walk into the kitchen, the chocolate globs hang from the ceiling, sweetly threatening to drop, but slowly hardening. Temporarily out of control, you spank the one kid who was trying to help, errant as it may have been. Guiltily, you then promise *you* will make some chocolate pudding, just as soon as you get one brother out of the tub, the other (who is now crying) out of the crib, and the chocolate off the ceiling.

The phone rings. You have just taken the littlest out of the crib, certain that his screams signal impending death or at best a lapse into a coma, which you wickedly think for a moment would be welcome silence.

Making your way to the phone, you hear a splash that can only be fatal for the middlest, left wrinkling in the lukewarm water. Littlest in hand, biggest in tow, you rush to the bathroom. There is nobody in the tub—only a naked, gleeful, and furless little monkey bending forward on the closed toilet seat, ready to practice yet another dive. You swat your second set of buns. The phone, meanwhile, has ceased ringing. You now find *yourself* sitting in the bathroom, glowering, wondering when Mommy will come home.

When the children ask why you aren't putting pajamas on them, you tell them that all big boys sleep in their underwear. This brilliant psychology leaves them feeling privileged, rather than neglected. Tucked into their beds, stories read, you slip out of the room.

"Mommy always leaves a glass of water on the desk," calls the biggest. During the trip downstairs in the dark, your tired feet find three die-cast metal cars, one Mr. Potato Head eye, and several jelly beans you gave them to pacify them before supper. The jelly beans stick to your feet, like huge corns. Surviving the obstacle course, you try in vain to remember why you came down.

Soon you are reminded by the biggest, who has come downstairs to get the water himself. You get the water. He says he's sleepy. He's tired. He says, "Carry me upstairs." Three hours earlier, forty-two pounds was nothing. Now it might as well be four hundred. However, you are a daddy, and daddies are strong, so up you go, jelly bean corns and all.

The littlest one is crying, so you bring him down and walk living room circles through reruns of "M*A*S*H*." He finally falls asleep halfway through "Nightline," so you make your hundredth trip up the stairs and lay him gently in his crib.

This is when you discover how beautiful they all are, each in his unique sleeping position. None of them look particularly dangerous; there is no threat to their even snoring. Like miniature contortionists, they have found what makes them comfortable for this moment. Each time you see them move, you utter a silent prayer that their eyes will remain closed until at least dawn.

Downstairs, you survey the combat zone. Confident you have won the war, you proceed to clean up the spoils of war: a partially eaten sandwich, a score of jelly beans, globs of chocolate pudding here and there.

Your supper uneaten, you take the green beans, all of the juice almost evaporated from sitting on the stove, and you munch out on what's left of them. The calories consumed are outmeasured by the ones you have already burned off.

Silently, you turn off the lights and make your final climb. All dieters need their rest.

2 Those Who Can Catch Get Tackled

I should have played football in high school, I guess. It doesn't matter that our school had over 2,000 students and a lot of them were macho male types whose only goal in life was dating cheerleaders. I still should have tried out and at least attended all the practices and warmed the benches.

My lack of pigskin prowess came back to haunt me after Zachary spent the afternoon at a baby-sitter's house the other day and came home devastated.

"They said I run funny," he wailed. "Besides that, the red-haired kid was acting like he was going to throw the ball to me and then threw it to someone else," he whined.

"And, when I did get the football and started to run, this big kid grabbed me and knocked me down and took it away from me," Zach screamed, outraged at the injustice.

I guess it is time for this father to explain the realities of football to a four-year-old who is big enough to play with the seven-year-olds but just not quite into tackle football.

That's life, Zach. Those who can catch can expect to be tackled. However, they can also expect some long gainers and a touchdown on occasion.

What I'm really trying to learn out of all this is how much "Like father, like son" will prevail in our house. After all, there are three sons, and we could not stand it if all are like father. Can you imagine the disgusting mountains of dirty socks that would pile up by the sides of the beds? Can you grasp the awesome task that the wife and mother of this clan would have if they all turned out to be as untrainable as I? It is definitely something we will have to work on, unless we want to turn our home into a kiddyland bachelor pad.

Children, it seems, do not have it particularly easy these days, although I suppose we never had it all that easy, either. Growing up is hard to do under the best of circumstances, and few circumstances are always best. Even in the land of delight that we paint for our children, there are lots of stumbles and grumbles along the way.

There's a lot of me that I want to pass along to Zachary, Russell, and Donovan, but I certainly wouldn't limit them to what I am. Like right now, Zachary wants to be a "working man." I get the subtle implication from the preschooler that I am not his idea of a "working man." Typewriters are not jackhammers. Writing stories is nothing, compared to building houses and fixing cars. He's just not into what his daddy is doing right now.

At home, Zach is trying to build a trailer house. So far, he has accumulated a lot of old wood, a few rusty nails, a diaper pail, and a stroller.

The diaper pail and stroller are essential items in any environment he has ever been in and were the obvious first furnishings for his home. He has declared he will live outside in the "trailer house" all alone when he is through building it, even though he still calls for me at night if he gets frightened in his darkened bedroom.

I am secretly dreading the day he no longer shares these nighttime fears with me, for it gives me one of those chances to redeem myself for not being the working man he visualizes. When I sit on the side of his bed and read his favorite stories, his fear disappears and my assuredness grows. Nobody reads stories like a man who loves words *and* kids.

Tomorrow morning, I'll head to the office and Zach will head to the "construction site," where we will each do our own things. We will both be busy men all day long, but tonight, before the sun sets, I will tour his trailer house and he will make a conciliatory gesture when he asks me, "What is it you do all day, Dad?" giving me the benefit of the doubt that, like the son, the father is a "working man."

3 Curious Clouds of Circus Dust

It was a cloudless night, and the temperature was cool for Oklahoma in late April. The fairgrounds were crowded with cars and vans parking on the grass, opening their doors and pouring forth excited children and skeptical adults. The carnival had come to town.

This would be the first carnival for my boys, and their voices rose to create an unbearable din at the sight of the one large tent with colored flags flying from around its top. Concession stands, a few small rides, and a group of weary-looking elephants greeted us as we walked on the dusty ground toward the booth where an almost toothless woman

sat dispensing tickets, perhaps dreaming of a day when she had been a top attraction at the carnival, high above the crowds in sequined tights and feathers.

In unison with hundreds of others, our feet kicked up a dusty cloud that reflected the lights of the carnival and hid the brilliant stars that had been visible from the parking lot. Hawkers pleaded for us to buy cotton candy or helium-filled balloons, or to visit trailers to see amazing reptiles or freaks of nature. I noticed that others, like us, passed the sideshows by. A poorly lettered sign showed that the price, seventy-five cents, had been marked out and fifty cents written in its place. A sad woman called to the crowds, but resignedly worked on an afghan, knowing they would not respond.

Before we entered the tent, I finished telling Zachary how, when I was a kid, I went to a carnival and won a big stuffed animal playing Pluck-a-Duck, where you pick up a duck from flowing water and the number on the bottom tells you if you have won a prize. This carnival tonight had no Pluck-a-Duck. It didn't have draglines, either. Remember those? For ten cents, you worked a crane, trying to pick up a prize from the bottom of a glass case. I never got the pocketknife or the watch, but always came up with a plaster-of-paris trinket.

A carnival with no ducks or draglines? I have to admit I was less than enthusiastic about entering the tent for the circus part of the affair.

For about the first fifteen minutes of the hour-long show, I chuckled to my wife about the ineptness of the circus's features. The trained dogs were sluggish. The monkeys looked old and weary, as did their trainer. I found little about the clown laughable. The tightrope walker seemed to shy away from anything really daring. Sadly, I realized that carnivals were being swallowed up in a world of synthetic excitement. How could they compete with video games, special-effects movies, Six Flags, and other wonders of science's love affair with entertainment?

Then I looked down at my boys. They were absolutely transfixed as a magician pulled a rabbit out of a hat and sawed a woman in two, only to put her back together again. They watched, fascinated, as a young acrobat pedaled a bicycle high overhead, precariously balanced on a rope. They shuddered with fearful glee as a beautiful girl flew through the air on a trapeze and was caught by a dashing young man. They laughed uncontrollably at the antics of a clown trying to start an antique car. They gasped as two trained poodles leapt through a ring of fire. And, finally, they clapped with frenzy as four elephants paraded around the circus ring grasping one another's tail in the grand finale.

We bought popguns—the old-fashioned toy with a cork on a string—and one Tweety-Bird on a stick for the baby, and drifted out into the night. There we saw a lot of familiar faces of parents, pooped after a carnival and a long day of work. They were ready to go home to bed. The other faces were of wide-eyed children who would also soon be in bed, dreaming of the circus. As children, they were still satisfied to be thrilled with what they had seen, rather than disappointed by what they had not. This night's carnival was unblemished by their memories of past ones.

"I want to be a magician when I grow up," announced Zachary, bringing me out of the clouds of memory. *At least it would be a safe occupation,* I mused.

"Or maybe a tightrope walker," he added.

"Me too," said Russell, not altogether sure what he was agreeing to.

Donovan played on innocently with his Tweety-Bird. I didn't respond to the other boys' dreams. If the dreams died, I wanted it to be at their own hands.

As we walked the carnival grounds, I noticed again that the stars were not visible in the sky. On this magical night, they were instead captured in a circus' neon lights and in children's eyes.

Weary as we were, we lingered there in the curious clouds of dust, unsure of what held us under the starless sky.

4 A Mother-in-law Is Not a Human

My mother-in-law flew in from Texas recently to visit her "adorable" grandchildren for a week. Now, before we get started, I want to make it clear this is no attack on mothers-in-law. I only use *mother-in-law* for descriptive purposes because it has more impact than just saying "Lisa's mother."

I like my mother-in-law for many reasons, not the least of which is that she will put the children to bed every night for this week, and she will do it with patience only the Beav's mother could approach. She will read storybooks I long ago decided were too long for bedtime. She will hum as she trudges up the stairs ten minutes after lights out with glasses of water all around. She will willingly wake up in the middle of the night to answer cries—and would sleep poorly if there were none. She will do all this with a smile on her face and still wake up ready to take walks and play in the sandbox.

My mother-in-law is not afraid of any messes, even the kind that have a mind of their own and seek you out no matter how desperately you flee. Nothing is too sticky for her to wipe away. No body is too dirty to be restored to a healthy pink glow. No shoes fall off too often. No fit is too furious.

In short, my mother-in-law is not human. At least, not in

the eyes of this parent. She makes us all look bad—and that's fine with me. After all, at week's end, she can get back on the plane and wave a teary-eyed good-bye. Meanwhile, the diapers will continue to do their thing. We'll take advantage of her until then.

We took her to a nice restaurant after meeting her plane, having left the adorables with the bravest sitter we could find. We made small talk over salads and apple fritters and slowly brought Grandmother up on the latest maneuvers and sly tricks up the six sleeves of her several grandsons. She responded with one of those looks that assures us she expects no trouble.

Over the main course, we discussed their good points: Zachary's "unbelievable" creativity, Russell's "incredible" intelligence, and Donovan's "absolutely amazing" communications skills for a two-year-old. She showed no surprise. After all, they are her grandchildren.

I was desperate during dessert. Wonderful as they are, I could think of nothing else to say, though nonparents may think that impossible. I tried politics. Silence. I tried business. Boring. I decided to just try eating.

"Well, aren't you even excited about the next one?" she asked. If you can imagine a smile of hurt excitement, that's what was on her face.

Cautiously, Lisa admitted she thinks mainly about the fourth baby when her pants get too tight or her breakfast doesn't set well or late at night when the other three are asleep. Other than that, she's pretty busy with two who are toilet training and one who is into wall painting.

I used this occasion—a perfect example of my expertise in poor timing—to throw in a quote I heard once about children. I knew my mother-in-law would be impressed.

"Parents are the bones on which children cut their teeth," I quoted Peter Ustinov.

She really wasn't overly impressed, so I tried to explain that I was feeling a little gnawed lately and it might have affected my sense of humor. Our kids' teeth are definitely in good condition, I pointed out. She pointed out that *kids* are baby goats, and our *children* are angels.

As we buckled our seat belts and prepared for a long week of childish indulgence, I fished for one more appropriate quote.

Glancing in the rearview mirror at my mother-in-law, I fairly whispered: "I've never been hurt by anything I didn't say." Then, like Calvin Coolidge, I shut up and listened to mother-daughter conversations with no further fatherly interruptions.

5 Shades of Black and White

I have an old black-and-white photo of me, my brother, and my two sisters in a city park in my hometown. We're posed on a swinging bridge over a dry creek under a hot summer sun.

I am seven years old, sporting a burr haircut and baggy shorts. At seven, there were many things about life I didn't understand yet, like why my father came only on weekends for trips to the park. I didn't understand divorce, but I sure got into the gifts he brought. On the day the photo was taken, he brought me a wooden puzzle with interchangeable facial features. Depending on my mood, the puzzle person could smile or laugh or cry.

I passed the puzzle on to my little sister, who, as the years passed by, passed it to someone else. "Daddy" became "Father." The park bridge was removed by a safety commission and weekends became busier, with both of us finding reasons not to get together.

We drifted apart. Letters became less frequent, phone calls fewer and shorter. After a while, I even had a problem visualizing what he looked like.

I remember, too, the awkwardness and distrust involved in welcoming a stepfather into our home. I wanted to be loyal to Dad, but I also longed to be friends with this man who was willing to take on the responsibility of teenagers he hadn't even fathered. After all, we weren't his fault. It was clearly a "Love me, love my kids," situation, and he accepted it with gusto.

He taught me about ratchet wrenches, how to change oil, tie a fishing lure, shoot a muzzle loader, put a fantastic shine on my car, respect women, love children, build a doghouse. What I'm trying to say is, he was there. Finally, someone was there.

This stepfather—I called him George—was a friend who taught me to like myself. It didn't matter whose son I was, only that I was me. If he gave me advice, he expected me to use it, if only for comparison. If he loaned me something, he expected it back. But, if he gave me something, he expected me to keep it.

I've kept the things George gave me, and I use many of them every day in dealing with my own three sons. Things you can't put a finger on, like time at the right time, encouragement with enthusiasm, and a firm touch.

Perhaps my best memory of George is the firmness of his handshake. I was nineteen when he told me point-blank I had to improve mine. A firm handshake, a good tight squeeze, and a straight look into another man's eyes, he said, puts you in control, or at least on an even footing. That's the way George and I approached each other.

I shook George's hand for the last time on the day he died. Only in his early fifties, losing a raging battle with cancer, he still squeezed as tightly as he could and searched for people's eyes. He was in control.

I miss both my fathers, for different reasons. One gave me life and the other showed me how to live it. One lives on in a small apartment in a tired Texas town. The other lives on in the memories of a younger father who greets peers with firm handshakes and teaches sons to tie fishing lures and build tree houses.

6 A Guilt-free Vacation

Planning a vacation soon? How about a little last-minute advice from the Hunter Travail Service? (No, that is not a misspelling.) *Travail* is defined as hard labor, and for many parents, that adequately describes vacations. The hard work we do all year in our jobs toughens us up enough to survive our family vacations.

Then there's the *real* vacation: The one where the kids go one direction and you go the other. No guilt—just glee. That's the kind we are discussing today. Following are a few basic suggestions for preparing for such a vacation.

- First, consult with vacation Bible school planners, Little League coaches, swimming teachers, soccer organizers, art and dance instructors, and possible birthday-party havers to make sure a summer vacation is even possible. Here's where you have to make your first tough decision. Will a couple of weeks out of their "summer development" curriculum harm your kids more than having their parents locked away for all's protection? This decision made, continue with your vacation planning.

• Contact grandparents well in advance to let them know when the children will arrive, explaining that the type of vacation you have in mind would be no fun for the kids. If they waver, tell them how little Susie wakes up nights calling for her grandpa. It'll work.

• Remember to tell the kids every day for two weeks in advance all the exciting things the grandparents have planned. Do this every time the kids begin asking what you will be doing on your vacation.

• Line up a responsible teenager to feed the fish and the dog, clean up the hamster cage, talk to the bird, water the plants, mow the lawn, turn on a few lights in the house occasionally, and assist if the cat delivers.

If you can't find such a teenager, let the lawn grow, give away the fish and the hamster, send the dog to Grandmother's with the kids, consider freeing the bird, donate the plants to the hospital, let lights burn out, and hope the cat has read up on natural childbirth.

• Carefully choose someone to pick up your mail. You want someone who will not ask questions about all the obviously past-due bills that are coming while you are blowing a wad on vacation.

• Make sure you have gathered all the favorite toys and blankets and put them in the right suitcase, so they end up at the right place. If you discover Billy Bob's blanket on Galveston Island while Granny's putting him to bed down on the farm, there'll be as many tears shed on the beach as on the homestead. Shipping that little blanket the next morning by air express may make the difference between staying in the Hotel Galvez or the Motel 6.

• About an hour before you leave on the vacation, comb the house for half-eaten peanut butter and jelly sandwiches. Look under the couch cushions for misplaced Milk Duds. Check the floor air conditioning vent behind the dining table for green beans that may have been hastily placed there when you were called to the telephone during dinner.

All of these items, if left alone, will change shape and aroma before you return, not to mention offering a feast for bugs. These same bugs are the ones who will stand solemnly on your front porch as you turn the corner in the family wagon. They will wave a foreleg in mock sorrow as they make plans to ravage the house. Six-legged hypocrites!

• One other thing. In the midst of getting traveler's checks, checking out the car, and being practical, don't forget to put clean sheets on the beds. You will all be so happy to get back home, you'll want to slide between the cool sheets and thank the stars over Galveston Island you're all back together again for another year. Having to put sheets on a bed can kill many a mood.

7

Oh, Woe Is She . . .

"Well, huddled masses, this man is yearning to breathe free," I said to my family Saturday morning over the Corn Flakes and Cocoa Puffs. "There're some things I would like to do today, and I would appreciate your cooperation. Please?"

"Can I help?" the oldest asked.

"Me too?" echoed the middlest.

"Sticky," said the third, shoving his jelly-covered hands into my face.

All in all, the responses had an ominous ring to them, particularly when measured against the silence of the lady who has promised to love, honor, cherish, and ignore my receding hairline. The look in her eyes on this up to now promising morning was clearly saying, "They're all yours, Dad."

My wife always reads what I write about children and always says, "Put your money where your mouth is." When I speak before groups about the importance of the father in the home, I usually say a necessity is "giving time at the right time." She had clearly decided this Saturday was as right as right could be. No plea for mercy can penetrate the cold eyes of a mother who responded twice in the night to calm monster dreams and once to cure an earache.

My fatal mistake—and what killed any hopes for sympathy—had been my ignoring our two-year-old when he

tugged on the covers at about 7:00 A.M., pleading for someone to come down and turn on the televison for cartoons. The poor guy had been afraid of the TV ever since someone left it on channel 40 (which is blank) and turned the volume all the way up. He had come in later, pulled the switch, and stood before the set, gripped in terror at the roaring static. Only after I switched it to familiar "Lassie" repeats was he able to breathe again. Even now, Russell touches no TV knobs.

I can always tell when my wife has decided the boys need their father. She starts talking about the new baby; the one due this fall. The one *she* is carrying up and down the stairs all day. The one that saps *her* strength, makes *her* feel nauseated. The one that sends *her* down in the middle of the night for crackers and milk. The one *she* sits through hours of doctor visits for, only to find out how much weight *she* has gained. The one *she* will go through labor for. Woe is *she*!

This morning she was able to communicate all that with a mere flicking of her cereal spoon and a weary glance down at the obvious protrusion around her middle. After all, for the third summer of our seven-summer marriage, the two-piece swimsuit would remain in the drawer in favor of one with a discreet skirt look and tanning lotion would be passed over for more stretch-mark-soothing lanolin. New curtains for the master bedroom would wait again, as she sews curtains for the new nursery.

I almost began to feel guilty: kind of a "look what you've done to her—again" feeling. Then she smiled and put down her spoon.

"I've got a compromise," she said. "Why don't we fill the pool and let the kids swim this morning? Then, after lunch, let's drive to the city and go to the zoo. The kids will sleep on the way, and we will have a chance to talk about plans for the new baby."

Suddenly, everything was resolved. The huddled masses would breathe free together. When I filled the pool, she oiled their bodies to guard against sunburn. Later, while I drained the pool, she sprayed their bodies to guard against the mosquitoes I bred last time I forgot to drain the pool.

After lunch, on the way to the city, all three of the little guys passed right out. It was peaceful, but we knew they were gathering strength. Only now came a change in our well-laid plans. Instead of talking about the baby-to-be, we talked about each other. And it sure was nice.

8 Some Books Belong on a High Shelf

My middlest son climbed to the top of our wall bookshelves to pilfer something off-limits to him. I caught him. The piles of books that had been moved to convert the shelves into a ladder gave him away.

While I put the books back on the shelves, I glanced at a few titles and reflected on how what we read tells a lot about who we are. Our shelves bear the weight of two sets of rarely touched encyclopedias. My heirs will still be paying for them after I have made my final journey. One shelf contains books on home repair for the novice—and the naive. The one on plumbing is water damaged. The one on home carpentry came very close to being sawed in half.

The books that really tell the tale are the ones on the fourth shelf, within easy reach. These are recommended reading for those on the marriage merry-go-round or the parental pathway.

- *Games People Play*—My wife-to-be and I fell in love in a discount store, arguing about the wisdom of my buying ten washrags for a dollar for my dorm room. She said they would come apart in the washing machine. I said I didn't intend to wash them anyway, but to buy ten new ones every two weeks, following every payday. Lots of marriages are made in heaven—a few at Bill's Discount Store.

• *Why Am I Afraid to Love?*—Six months after falling in love, I began to see the consequences. We did our laundry together on Friday nights. Something about our blue jeans tumbling in the same dryer was very foreboding.

• *The Secret of Staying in Love*—This one was a gift from my new mother-in-law. After seven years, I still haven't read it, but if I feel the need, I will. If I see Lisa reading it first, though, I'm going to panic.

• *Why Natural Childbirth?*—This one is really worn, and we are considering either purchasing a new copy or writing our own sequel entitled, *"More Natural Childbirth—Why Me?"*

• *Thoroughly Married*—There's nothing like three kids asking questions in your laps as you watch the tenth rerun on television of your favorite courtship movie, *The Way We Were.* We know we're thoroughly married; this book just makes us know we aren't alone.

• *Toilet Training in Less Than a Day*—It took two men with Ph.D.s to write this book, several long evenings to read it, and about six months to train our first son. It's all worth it, though, to hear those gleeful words: "I went pee-pee in the potty!"

• *The Jungle*—This book used to be on another shelf. It's one saved from a high-school English course. I reread it after our third child learned to walk, thinking it might put our home's condition in better perspective. With a little federal aid, I really think we could turn things around pretty quickly.

• *530 Vital Questions Every Mother Asks About Her Child's Health*—I read the whole book and still wasn't prepared when Russell put nickels up his nose. Besides that, the book is stereotyping by making the assumption fathers don't give a darn about their child's health. Ain't so, is it fellow dads?

• *The Total Woman*—I shivered every time I saw Lisa pick this one up. I knew I loved her, but I wasn't sure I wanted even more of her. What if I didn't like the total? No regrets.

• *Your Blood Pressure: The Most Deadly High*—A gift from my mother after we visited her and brought all the grandchildren. Since reading, I've cut down on salt, begun exercising again, and may yet survive sons-strain.

• *The Boys and Girls Book About Divorce*—Don't know where this one came from, but reading it is enough to convince you to recall, "I do take thee for richer, for poorer, for better, for worse, in sickness and in health, to love, to honor . . . and forsaking all others to keep myself only unto you . . . to have and to hold from this day forward until death us do part."

There were lots of other books, but my attention turned to Russell, and I finally asked what he was after in the first place. A book, of course.

• *Daddy and I Do . . .*—This is Russell's favorite. It tells simple little stories about what daddies do with their boys. It's my favorite, too, and that's why I keep it on a high shelf—so he won't read it without me.

9 "You Must Be Very Proud"

"Oh, what adorable little boys. Are they yours?"

"No, ma'am. Actually, I'm an undercover agent assigned to track them. They're really three very dangerous criminals escaped from exile in the Soviet Union. We're not really sure what they're after yet, but I'm working on it."

"You must find your work very rewarding," responded the little, round, white-haired lady with soft, pudgy fingers as she bent over to tweak their cheeks.

"Be careful, ma'am. They bite," I warned, and she shuffled away through the doors of McDonald's, never to be seen again, muttering something about discipline, truth, and the American Way. I returned to my hamburger and my anxieties. We're on vacation. This is our fifth meal on the road, and the novelty has worn off.

"Three boys? You must be very proud." Another grandmother has stopped at our table, all sweetness and light, oblivious to the threatening looks on the faces of the boys, whose cheeks are overtweaked and foreheads chapped from passing kisses.

"Well, actually I'm just their agent," I responded. "They're a circus act. We're on our way to a performance in the big top now, and they're practicing. That's why they sit on top of the table. They're acrobats. It's sad, really. They were abandoned in the jungles of Africa by a Swedish expedition. They look sweet, but they're really quite dangerous."

"Poor little dears," she said with tears in her gentle eyes. "Maybe I can catch their act."

"You just did," I sighed, as one juggled pickle slices, another blew bubbles in his chocolate shake, and the third squeezed a ketchup packet in her direction. She fled, but there was forgiveness in her eyes.

Soon they were strapped into their seat belts, which keep them safe from the road and keep me safe from them, and we headed down the interstate. Ten different toys in the backseat, and they all wanted the same one. Thirty minutes of hair pulling, screaming, hitting, and kicking pass as they slowly settle down for the afternoon nap, which should be good for 100 miles at least.

"I need to go to the potty."

"You went at lunch," I growled in a threateningly understanding voice.

"I need to go again," he whimpered.

"You'll have to wait."

"I can't." The whimper had changed to defiance.

He was right. He couldn't—and didn't.

The mother of these mini-machos awoke just as they all fell into slumber. She had fallen asleep reading about Robert Redford in *Redbook*, completely oblivious to the backseat battalions waging war with pillows and Oreo cookies.

"I sure could use a rest stop," she said pleasantly.

"We've only gone forty miles since lunch," I cried (almost literally).

"Well, I *am* pregnant," she answered. Somehow, looking into the rearview mirror at our three blond time bombs, I found her words less than reassuring.

Late that night, under the full Texas moon, having crammed a seven-hour drive into twelve hours, we arrived at Pop's and Grandmother's. Having spent the last three hours remembering the births of our babies, as they slept

quietly, we arrived in one of our proudest parental moods.
"How was the trip?" There was caution in Pop's question.
"It was perfect."
"And the kids?"
"Just great."
"You must be very proud."
"Right. Good night."

10 No One Knits Anymore

It's an old familiar woe: the husband who forgets his wedding anniversary and ends up sleeping on the couch or in the doghouse with Fido's fleas. How come tradition says the man has to remember the anniversary? After all, he had the burden of the proposal, too.

Sunday was our anniversary, and I did not forget. How can I? My mind now equates anniversaries with maternity clothes. Tradition holds that we stop for the monthly maternity checkup at the doctor's office on the way to our evening out. We hold hands around the candlelight in romantic restaurants and discuss the pros and cons of saddling the "young uns" with family names to please the grandpas. Traditionally, we leave the restaurant early enough to walk the shopping center and window-shop for crib toys or baby booties. No one knits anymore, it seems.

Remember on TV or in old movies, how the father found

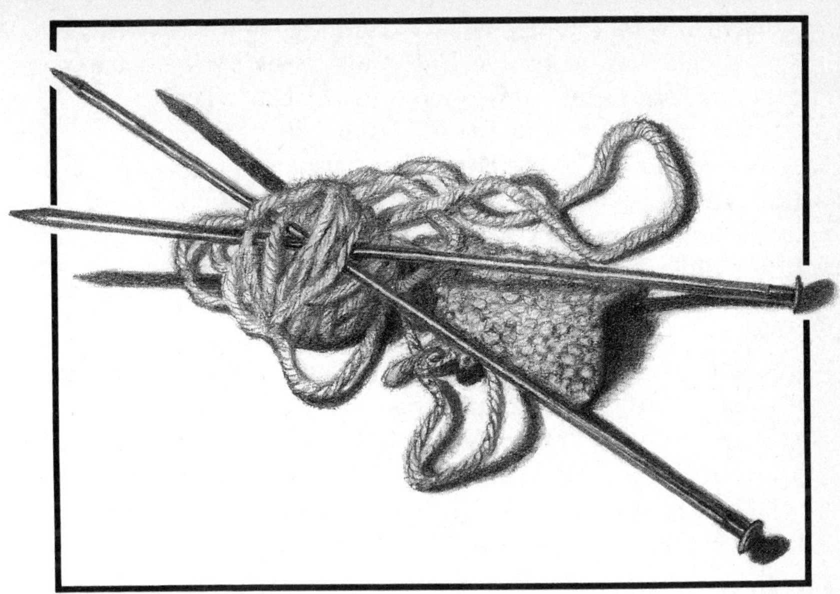

out his wife was pregnant when she suddenly started knitting blue or pink booties or blankets? Now the father, in a panic, rushes to the drugstore for a special kit to verify fears or substantiate hopes. Times change. While it's still exciting to feel the baby kick, you can go to the doctor and have a sonogram and get a picture of him, or her, inside the womb long before birth.

"Yep, he's really in there," was all I could say. "Search real good for twins. Just in case," I told the nurse. One lonely little floater was all she found.

"Don't you worry, little feller, you've got a welcoming committee that could overpopulate Rhode Island already," I joked.

Come November, I'll cut my fourth umbilical cord. I've always searched out tolerant doctors who grasp the significance of the father's role. For the second time, I will be allowed to actually deliver the baby, with the doctor standing by and ready. Like I said, times change.

Three years ago, my wife and I celebrated our anniversary in a Dallas heat wave. She could barely walk. The next morning, she awoke refreshed and went into labor. I got a day off from work and a second son.

Two years ago, we celebrated our anniversary in an Oklahoma heat wave. Our third son wasn't born until ten days later, holding out for cooler weather, probably on the advice of his older brother.

Our first son had chosen a February snowstorm. I seriously considered fitting Lisa with skis to get her to the hospital, but it was downhill all the way, and the car made it. That was definitely better than the time we stopped at a grocery store with her well dilated but me hungry for cookies. Our car wouldn't start, so we walked to the hospital. It was only about six blocks or so, but they rushed her quickly into the labor room and we soon had Russell.

So, how did we celebrate our anniversary Sunday? We started Saturday. We spent the evening reminiscing about the births of our children, talking about names, discussing changes for the nursery decoration, and wishing Donovan would be potty trained before the new arrival. It was a beautiful evening. After all, having babies is one of the things we've been best at in the seven years we've been married.

The Saturday discussion left us free Sunday evening to sit in the romantic restaurant and talk of ourselves, reminisce about our wedding, and gaze into each other's eyes. It was hard to break tradition, but we managed—almost. Until Lisa looked at her watch.

"If we hurry, we can make it to the store before it closes," she said softly.

"You're right," I agreed. "What do we need?"

"I was hoping to find a pair of yellow booties, maybe on sale?"

She glowed as we paid the check. With three boys at home, yellow booties seemed a logical and safe compromise, but we also picked up a soft pink blanket—and kept the receipt. It was a happy anniversary.

11 "We Hold These Truths to Be Self-evident . . ."

"Dad, what's abortion?" My five-year-old dug his toes in the dirt and twisted the ball in his baseball mitt. He might have been nervous, but his gaze was as direct as his question.

"Uh . . . ready to play baseball?"

"Oh, yeah, Dad. Only first, what's abortion?"

When I was five, I know I was much more likely to ask what a B-52 bomber was, or why the waves stayed in the ocean, or why birds flew and bees stung. My daddy could have sat me on his knee and answered those questions to my satisfaction without so much as a gasp of alarm or a smidgen of self-doubt.

I looked at my son, a mere baby he seemed, but one who has heard something somewhere about abortion and wants his daddy to tell him what he heard wasn't true. I wondered briefly where he heard it. Was it pro or con? In his little but mighty mind, how much does he already know? Where is the innocence we acquaint with big-eared little boys who can one moment put on a cape and leap about saving civilization as a superhero, and then drop the cape and, puzzled, ask about abortion?

Wasn't it just the other day I pointed to his mommy's stomach and explained that there was a baby in there that would in a few months be another little brother or, perhaps, even a little sister? He asked questions then, too. "How does it eat?" "Does it like to swim in there?" "Is it already a person?"

I said it eats all the time, loves to swim in there, and yes, most definitely, is a person already. Just like he was when he was that small. Just like his two brothers were. Just like we all were.

Now he wants to know what abortion is.

"Why do you want to know about abortion?"

"Well, Michael said his mother said that if she were in Mommy's shoes and had three little kids already and another one on the way, she'd get an abortion instead of another baby. Will Mommy trade in the new baby for an abortion after it's born?"

Suddenly, I *really* wanted to play baseball, but I knew I had to explain. As gently as I could, I told Zach how an abortion isn't a trade at all, but that it is something that is done to keep a baby from being born at all.

"But Mommy can't get an abortion, right? 'Cause you said the baby is already a person inside her," said Zach, clearly glad he wasn't going to have to worry about that anymore.

"Well, Zach, she still could if she wanted to, but she won't, because she doesn't want to at all."

"And you wouldn't let her, would you?"

I thought about how even death-row prisoners convicted of murder and rape get automatic appeals before the execution is carried out; how they have the right to a lawyer, an advocate to plead their case individually. I had already said the unborn baby is alive—a person. I had also explained that he could still be aborted. How could I explain that laws don't offer him the right to a defense? I decided not to try, but to turn once again to baseball. We walked slowly.

"Gosh, Dad. I'm glad Mommy didn't decide to have an abortion instead of Russell, Donovan—or me. I'd miss 'em."

"Me, too, Zach. Me, too. Now, let's play ball. I'll pitch. You hit."

"One more thing, Dad. It seems like everybody ought to at least get to be born. To be a baby."

"I know, Zach. That's what the Declaration of Independence says."

"The what?" Instead of waiting for an answer, he headed for home base to wait for a pitch.

I wouldn't have been able to quote it, but I looked it up later:

"We hold these truths to be self-evident, that all men are created equal, that they are endowed by their Creator with certain inalienable Rights, that among these are Life. . . ."

12 Leaps Have Limits, but Dreams Do Not

Dear Boys:

There's something you ought to know about your father: He loves you. Not only in a greeting card fashion under an autumn sunset by a golden pond. Not only in a telephone company commercial, making amends over haircut arguments and adolescent responsibility. He loves you always.

To the biggest: I loved you this morning when you got on that big yellow school bus for the first time ever after crossing the yard, heading down the driveway, picking up speed as you approached the door. I loved you when you didn't look back at me, but greeted the other riders with a "Gimme five." You always take on new things that way. Tonight you'll tell me all about it with the right mixture of bravado and humility. Today kindergarten, tomorrow the world.

To the middlest: You turned three this month and saw your older brother head off to school. Might I call you a monkey? You never had the curls of your brothers to hide your ears, as they do. Thinner than they, it has been a particular delight of mine to watch you, almost spidery, make your way around the house, vanquishing whatever foes may enter your imagination. Whenever you've lacked courage, you've drawn on imagination. While others may take a leap, you can describe one as if you had, while keeping your feet firmly planted. You seem already to have learned that leaps have limits and dreams do not. In you, I sometimes see me, and I think we could stand to practice our leaping together, like we share our dreaming.

To the littlest: You turned two this month. Two and tiny, but two and tough. For longer than the others, we've allowed your baby hair to lay around your collar, the curls catching sunlight and sand, sometimes glistening with little-boy sweat, sometimes shimmering with shampoo, sometimes knotted with jelly or tangled from play. Finally, no one mistakes you for a little girl. You have mastered the language, progressing from "blankey" and "mine" to being able to request dinner on time. You are the protester, demanding fairness for all and particularly for you. I watch how you watch me, so intense for someone so recently created, as if you are making mental notes on items to discuss later for possible improvements. And then I hear you say "MY DADDY!" in a voice mixed with both awe and acceptance. I wish that I would always awe you, but the world takes on that task.

This letter to you, sons, is not a behind-the-back way of

letting you know that your "gruff old dad" does love you. You know I love you, just as clearly as you know that your dear old dad just isn't that gruff. Besides, none of you can read yet, so the letter's not really to you, anyway. It's just that I don't think people always give fathers credit for all the love they have inside for sons and daughters.

I read recently about fathers who don't pay child support, about fathers who abandon their children completely, about fathers who beat their children, about fathers who ignore their children, about fathers who "push" their children, about fathers who use their children, about fathers who disown their children, about fathers who are embarrassed by their children—about fathers who never learn to say "I love you."

Sometimes you see a movie about a father who loves his child enough to fight for him and change for him, but you know they made the movie because they think the story is so exceptional. But I can't help wonder who sets the standards for exceptions and why people decide so-and-so is a good daddy because he acts like a mommy. Maybe we've gotten too descriptive in this generation; we have "providers," and "breadwinners," and "father figures," and "role models," when what we really need is "daddies."

We need good men who love good little boys and good little girls, so we can all feel good. I thought of that this morning when you, Russell, pressed your face to the front-door glass as I left for work and said, "Be good, Daddy." I said I would. You said you would, too, and we both believed each other.

Sons, you've got a long way to go. Right now, I see among you an explorer, a writer of dreams, and a judge. The world may someday applaud your success, just as someday it may realize there's a lot of good daddies out there, too.

With love,
Your father

13 I'm Not a Mother. I'm Your Wife!

Today's my wife's birthday. She considers it pretty special, I suppose, so she wasn't too thrilled with me when I sprung some advance mathematics on her. If you figure there are about 240,000,000 people in this country, there's a fair chance that 657,534.25 of them are celebrating their birthdays today. Kind of takes the "my day" feeling away. Hard to feel like "Queen for a Day" when there's enough birthday girls to form an Amazon queendom.

I personally know of at least one other birthday today—my mother-in-law. Like mother, like daughter, I suppose. It's the time of the year I am most sympathetic to my father-in-law's plight. For twenty-two years, they were both his responsibility.

Lisa said, back in March when she began to think about her birthday coming up, that she didn't want me to make a big deal over it this year. So, she decided in April, thinking ahead of January snows, that she wanted an automatic garage door opener for her birthday in September. I told her I would consider oiling the hinges.

Her birthday wishes throughout the summer have fluctuated along with the bank balance. Let me tell you, that's fluctuation. In June, I could have gotten away with just a promise to clean the fish aquarium. You see, we—well, I—having a flare for the exotic, had bought a "blue lobster" for the aquarium, thinking the kids would enjoy something a little more vicious than Goldie. Alas, poor Goldie. She was the first to fall prey to the lobster, which proceeded to eat four neons, a loach, something I can't pronounce, and then, lacking any morals at all, the angelfish. Lisa wouldn't go near the aquarium. I could have gotten off economically by cleaning the lobster lair.

July provided a little brighter economic picture, as we found a huge stash of pennies in Zachary's bedroom. Seems he had taken liberties with dear old Dad's pockets when dear old Dad draped his pants across the easy chair and retired to bed. Zach kept the change in a peanut butter jar that was still half-filled with peanut butter and missing a lid. We judged from the amount of mold that there could be a considerable amount of money there. Lisa said she'd clean it up if I would take her out to dinner with some friends and get her a romantic Hallmark card.

I should have agreed. We ended July in the black, barely, but it might as well have been financial midnight. All of a sudden, she wanted nightgowns, *plural.* Granted, at six months pregnant, and normally being fairly thin, she looks a little like a garden hose with a large mouse stuck inside. Remember those cartoons? I told her she looked just fine to me. She pouted all day and threatened to sew up the sides of the camping tent for a new nightie.

August brought the county fair and memories of her tragic loss there last year of her wedding ring. After six years of glittering on her little hand, it fell off somewhere and was trampled into the dusty ground by a big old steer, or found later by someone with a metal detector on a particularly lucky day. I offered to buy her a "mother's ring."

"A mother's ring!" she exclaimed. "I am not a mother. I am your wife!" Never mind the fact our fourth child is very obviously imminent.

I call my wife every day from the office, long-distance, just to cheer her up. She told me yesterday that the carpet cleaners are coming today to do all the rooms. "I decided that's what I want for my birthday," she said. And I said fine, as long as they can get the Play-Doh out of the entryway.

She'll still get a cake, dinner with friends, and a Hallmark. I'm going to save the nightgown for a couple more months.

Next year, Lisa turns thirty (*now* I'm in trouble), and I assume she'll want to ignore that birthday. I'll know for sure next March, when she starts gearing up.

14 At the End of the Rainbow

People sometimes stop me in the hallways at church and tell me how blessed I am. Last week a grandfather held me at bay in a hardware store for fifteen minutes, talking about how much he misses his grandsons. While we talked, my three sons tried out tools, chiseling little dents in the tile floor. The smallest one headed out the front door with a set of jumper cables, saying he was going to "fikit," meaning the car.

I was about to make the kind gentleman an offer he couldn't refuse when he spotted a cute little blonde about two years old, in full Strawberry Shortcake regalia. He lost interest in me and my sons. By this time, the oldest had

used a screwdriver to loosen the ends of a metal shelf supporting a paint display. Yes, I am blessed.

Generally, people regard me as a patient father, one who keeps smiling all the way to the car, where my fury breaks loose. Even then I am generally restrained. Want to know how we "blessed fathers" do it? We search arduously for the pot of quiet at the end of the turbulent rainbow.

Sometimes it is a long journey, but it's there. You have to depend on psychological mood elevators. For you sophisticates, let me make myself clear: I do not mean drugs. In most cases, aspirin is no more effective than Reese's Pieces when it comes to dealing with in-house aliens (your children).

Children do make life complicated, so I would suggest you look for joy and calm in the simple things around you. These things work when you are in need of knowing you are still *you*, in spite of all *them.* Knowing you are still you will make you a better you for them. Right?

Some of these things work for me:

• Those few days of Oklahoma fall when it is just cool enough to leave the windows open and the heater and air conditioner off. Take a lawn chair out and watch the electric meter move ever so slowly. What glee.

• A real, live, handwritten letter from a real, live person you really like.

• White peppery chicken-fried-steak gravy, with no lumps, poured over biscuits and surrounded by ripe tomatoes from your own garden—the only vegetables that survived the heat.

• A few lines from an old poem that suddenly pop into your mind: "Two roads diverged in the wood, and I—I took the one less travelled. . . ." You could write your high school English teacher a thank-you note, if you have the time.

• A genuine smile from someone who you thought didn't even know you existed.

• Climbing into bed tired and realizing your wife washed the sheets and dried them in the sun, catching a bit of heaven in the folds.

• Three little blond boys playing in a sandbox outside in the backyard with faded plastic shovels that were new at the beginning of summer. You ponder the approaching autumn from the safe confines of your easy chair, behind double-paned windows. So quiet.

• Being called by name by someone you didn't realize even knew it—someone you always wanted to get to know better.

• A young couple at church who can't contain their excitement because they are going to have a baby. Boy, that one makes you smile, doesn't it?

• One of those huge American flags brightly lit at night and visible from a mile away, with enough breeze to make it fly. I like the joy of freedom.

• Driving alone at sunset with the radio up high and a

disc jockey who plays only the songs I can sing along with. No one's listening, and I think I'm pretty good.

• A call from a mechanic who says, "It was just a loose belt. No charge."

• A box of pictures pulled out from under the bed, and plenty of time to look at them.

• Untangling little-boy bodies from bed sheets, pulling covers up to chins, whispering good night, closing doors, saying prayers, and going to sleep. Night after night, followed by day after day. *Joy.*

15 Not My E.T. Tennis Shoes!!

I wouldn't grow up again if my life depended on it. It was hard enough the first time around: the experiences of being too pudgy, too skinny, too slow, too rowdy; wanting things I couldn't have sometimes, getting things I didn't want sometimes; choosing the wrong role models sometimes, having the wrong role models forced on me sometimes. Man, those were some times!

This is the year I turn thirty, but it is also the year my oldest son turns six. I think I would rather be thirty. At least I have lots of excuses for who I am. Little old Zach's got a lot of choosing yet to do, and hopefully, a lot of rejecting to do as well.

When I was a kid, I can remember buying clothes. What I

wore was not dictated by fashion. No way. What I wore was on sale. If J. C. Penney's was featuring green corduroy, I might have to wear it all year—with yellow plaid shirts, if they were in the basement sale at Sears. Tennis shoes were either black or white, high top or low, and had to last at least half the year, so I could get new shoes for Christmas. All my socks were white because they would go with anything on sale anywhere and also with black or white tennis shoes. Kids, by the way, had no accessories.

Zachary's closet looks like a rainbow factory. He lays his clothes out at night to make sure they match. And, just in case he is different from the other boys at school, I discreetly check. They're also fashion coordinated, for the most part. In 1960, when I was in first grade, jeans were jeans, stiff and hard with double knees and cuffs for growing space. Now jeans are either "501s" "or they ain't jeans." At least not for public viewing, anyway.

It's a modern commercial sin, really, for the designers to make miniature clothes the way they do. I work all day, and my son dresses better for play than I do for an important social event. Then you have well-meaning advisers who tell you to buy the bargains and make the kid wear them. You know, it gives them strength of character and all that. But what do you do when your five-year-old sulks into the living room, plunks down on the couch, and says, "No matter what TV says, plain pockets are out. So are Smurf underpants, and I need to replace my E.T. tennis shoes—today?"

It could be worse, I guess. I remember in the fifth grade I had a friend whose mother sewed all his clothes. He looked great to all the other mothers, including mine. She decided to make me some shirts—you know, save all that money. She dug through her material and made the oddest looking pink shirt. I looked like a walking sheet for a honeymoon suite. I hid her thread, buried her needles, and became at least a little fashion conscious myself.

It's fine for children to be more aware of the world around them. I'm all for that. Five-year-olds know now that sweat makes them smell bad, and they want deodorant. They choose their toothpaste and point out to smokers that they are killing themselves and the whole world around them. As a parent, I do wish five-year-olds could be a mite more tactful. For instance, we have come to accept the fact that the mom at our house is a little big these days because she's pregnant. Now, when we shop, Zachary carefully surveys all the larger ladies and in his best stage whisper asks me, "Is she pregnant, or is she fat?" There's no good answer for that one, guys.

Don't think I don't appreciate my son. I've never been good at putting things together for that "well-coordinated look." I've been considering having Zachary wake up a little earlier in the morning and go through my closet, pulling out a shirt, pants, and tie for me to wear, just like Mommy did when I was his age. If I can get Zach's approval, I'll go out each day and conquer the world, just like he does. Of course, he might gasp at the grayness of the closet and the simplicity of styles. The saddest thing of all is that he would probably make me throw out my E.T. tennis shoes. You know; like son, like father.

16 The Chocolate-Almond Reward

With a little practice, grooming, and patience, we men can do almost all the stereotypical jobs of housewife and mother.

In other words, if you're in a situation where Mom brings home the bacon, you, Dad, should be able to cook it. If the wife inhabits the executive suite, the husband must be able to save the kitchen from yellow waxy build-up. And while I have no doubts we men are prepared to wear the aprons in the family, here, for you, is my very incomplete guide to help men prepare in advance for the days of house husbandry that may lie ahead.

• *Diapers*—If you have small children, buy disposables. Tell your wife it is for her benefit, because you hate to see her doing all that laundry. Actually, it is a precaution for the day she stays sick in bed, becomes the major breadwinner, goes away for the weekend on a retreat, or refuses to change one more diaper. If you get stuck with the diaper changing, you don't want pins to worry about. They don't work—even if you *do* run them through your hair first.

Don't think you have to enjoy changing diapers just because you love your kids. It is never pleasant. I once knew a lady in the church nursery who said, "Here, dear, I don't mind." I started to recommend professional counseling.

• *Housecleaning*—I use the "neat pile" approach. It conveys to people that your cleaning is in process, instead of admitting to people you don't know where everyone's clothes are kept or whose shirts and underwear are whose.

If you have a portable dishwasher, *never* forget to turn on the water before you wash. Talk about baked-on debris! Lisa came close to getting a new set of dishes the first time I washed the old ones.

If you live in a two-story house and your vacuum cleaner has wheels, be careful that the cord doesn't get around your leg on the stairs. I once ended up at the bottom with a busted bag and vacuum hose almost up my nose. The kids stood at the top of the stairs laughing until the cloud of dust almost eliminated them.

• *Cooking*—Men naturally make better cooks than women. Haven't you heard? Our grilled cheeses have more cheese, more butter, more calories. Our peanut butter and jelly sandwiches are superb. By the way, it is better if you put peanut butter on one piece of bread and jelly on the other, and then put them together. This method keeps the jars pure, which is obviously a low priority for many women.

My two main cooking mistakes have been trying to cook from scratch and not reading directions carefully. I doubled the water once in an angel food cake and could have sold the results to the developers of Silly Putty. I also cooked a soufflé under the broiler once and tried to pass it off as a cheese soup with a top crust. Didn't pass.

• *Grocery shopping*—I'm pretty good at this, though it takes me two hours or more to read all those price symbols on the shelves. I'm not all that good at math and usually end up with the brand names I know best. But, because I handle the grocery shopping about half the time, we have discovered frozen burritos, chocolate-almond ice cream, Fruit Roll-Ups, Pop-Tarts, Hawaiian bread, and expanded waistlines. And no, it doesn't help to eat before you go shopping. That only makes you want dessert.

Shopping *is* educational. While in line, you can read all the headlines on those trashy newspapers the store sells. Only problem is, you don't get to share the headlines at the beauty salon.

• *Putting children to bed*—First comes the bath. At my house, you put three dirty little bodies in one big tub, throw in a bar of soap, and make them all mad at one another. They wash one another pretty well.

If you can't find pajamas, let them sleep in their underwear. They'll love you for it, especially if that's the way you sleep. Throw them in bed, threaten them with their lives if they get up again, head for the chocolate-almond, and ignore the noises coming from their room for the next two hours.

Remember, this list is far from complete. Mommy's work is never done!

17 I Couldn't Find the Humor

I'd like to tell my kids that it is an always beautiful world in which they live and that things always turn out all right in the end, that the good guy wins and the rain falls just as much on the unjust. But I also like to be honest. And yesterday on the news I learned that the Russians shot down a passenger airplane with 269 people aboard, babies included. I wish I could tell my kids that life is always okay. Yes, Virginia, and there's never been a dry well in Oklahoma.

"Some days are diamonds. Some days are stone." And today is a day for putting away the sense of humor and dwelling momentarily on the unfun. It's the least I can do for those who died.

On television news this morning, they showed two Japanese searchers walking along a beach in a pouring rain, searching for debris. My oldest son was fascinated with the rain-soaked men and asked me what they were doing. I told him. He then asked me why the plane was shot from the sky. I couldn't tell him why. Oh, I repeated the Russian propaganda—their reasons—but this only left him puzzled, like the majority of civilized people.

This reminded me of an earlier time, when he asked me if punch was poisonous. He had heard on television about a man named Jim who had served red punch to his "people," and they had all died. I had a difficult time explaining that one, too.

Somehow, I fail at explaining the inhumanity of man to my children. I warn them about children who disappear, but they look at me with disbelief as I sing them songs and tuck them in at night. I've seen them crash toy airplanes in the sandbox or drop bombs from make-believe jets on make-believe towns. It's all make-believe.

What I don't like is telling them how much of their make-believe really happens in a world full of older and "wiser" humans: telling them bombs are real, and that while some planes fall from the skies, others are shot from them. Their definition of *hurt* is a scraped knee, a finger smashed in a door, a fall from a tree house, a bee sting. In the emotional realm, they are crushed by a too harsh word from a parent or too much teasing from a friend. A hug or an apology is a catchall cure, so far.

But they do have nightmares. This is a sure sign their innocence has vanished like birds before a storm. It is almost as if they know there's a lot of pain yet unrealized, a lot of reality yet to confront, a danger in growing, a futility in learning to practice self-control in a world so often out of control.

So often we parents, we fathers, are called upon to tell a child all's right with the world. That a kiss will cure a bruise. That a little sugar will make the medicine go down, and a smile can be your umbrella. That the rain falls on the wicked and the sun shines on the good. That the Golden Rule still works and there is justice for all.

And then there are other times, those more challenging ones. Explaining cancer. Helping someone understand why someone else lies. Pointing out that man places limits on all things, including love, truth, and justice. It's not easy, but it's parenting.

I understand now why we are born as babies. When we're babies, human faces are only joyful to look upon. Pain is never expected.

I'm thankful my children cannot read. As a writer, I know that words bear news they're not yet ready to bear. I'm thankful their innocence yet works as a filter for the bad and a vacuum for the good, because I like the balance this allows.

You know, it would be a lot easier to be a father if you did not love your children so. Maybe that's why there's so much bad news these days. There's just too little love. For some reason, I just can't find the humor in that, no matter what anyone says.

I hope you don't mind just this once. It seems the least I can do.

18 Is That a Cold Coming On?!!

In the interest of equal time, I frequently remember to talk about mothers. After all, they are somewhat responsible for the way the children turn out. If I can only bring home beans, she'll boil them; if I bring home steak, she'll broil it. We are a team.

Without getting into a deep debate about "societal roles," I maintain that there are definite differences between mothers and fathers. It's part of our makeup, which, by the way, mothers wear. Most fathers I know don't. There are some other differences that you may already have noticed. Among them:

- Mothers like to call other mothers on the telephone and visit about things like potty training and diaper rash and whether their sons ought to be allowed to take dance lessons. Fathers don't talk about these subjects much—especially the dance lessons for their sons.
- Mothers love to play charades at parties with other couples. The urge comes from spending days trying to guess what children are really saying. Fathers don't like charades. They like pretzels and "Monday Night Football."
- Fathers like dogs, and mothers like cats. Neither like hamsters, but they put up with them because the kids do.
- Mothers can turn away door-to-door salesmen before

the doorbell stops ringing. Fathers end up with encyclopedias, multitudes of magazines, lifetime light bulbs, lots of cookies, and Blue and Gold Sausage. Fathers have developed a skill for turning down vacuum cleaners, however.

• Fathers, no matter how muscular, lack the ability to keep their clothes from piling up on the floor. They are just too weak to pick them up. Mothers, on the other hand, pick up clothes all over the place.

• Mothers who are home during the day like to take afternoon naps each weekday. Fathers who are at work during the week like to take afternoon naps on the weekends. Mothers don't like fathers to take afternoon naps on the weekends.

• Mothers generally end up taking little ones to the rest room in public places, no matter what sex the little ones are. Fathers say this is because the mother is accustomed to being in the rest room twenty minutes anyway. Mothers with sons look forward to the day when the sons can no longer go to the women's rest room.

• Mothers like toilet seats left down. Fathers don't really care, but they always forget to leave them down. Mothers think this is on purpose.

• Mothers like to experiment with teas, surprising the family with mint and spice and orange and lemon pekoes, or something like that. Fathers like tea in big glasses with lots of ice and sugar.

• Mothers like salad lunches with the girls. (That's considered to be a derogatory term, I understand.) Fathers like salads with their pizza at the noon buffet. And, on the subject of salads, mothers like carrot salad. Fathers don't. It's never served at home, but always available at the cafeterias.

• Mothers summon more strength when they become sick with a cold or the flu. They work harder to keep things caught up around the house, just in case someone else in the family gets sick and they have to take care of them. Fathers with colds are bedridden instantly and in great need of mothering. Weakness overtakes them. They can't even change the television dial or fluff up their pillows. They take their temperature every twenty minutes and review their life-insurance policies.

• Mothers stop at service stations if the car smells hot, a tire looks low, or they think they may be lost. Fathers know better. They let the car overheat, change the flat on the side of the highway, and get lost in the wilderness.

• Mothers don't like to be stereotyped the way I just did here. Fathers don't like it, either. I should know, because I'm not at all like the guy above. Not one little bit. I hope I get through the day, though, because I feel a cold coming on.

19 When God Made These Hands . . .

You probably haven't heard what a great handyman I am. When God made these hands, He broke the mold. Or I did, trying to hang it on the wall. I should hang my tools on the wall and leave them there; they and everyone else would be safe. Problem is, I can't find my tools.

My wife yearns for a handyman, and our house fairly cries out for one. I grew up in the city, in apartment buildings. If something broke, you called the manager. If he didn't fix it, you moved to another apartment building and hoped you'd get your deposit back. When we bought our

house, we moved in and—armed with two *Reader's Digest* guides promising to make me into a first-class handyman—I felt prepared to do all those things my dad never taught me and the shop teacher almost keeled over trying to teach me back in high school.

Those two large books have come in handy. I used them once to apply pressure when I tried to glue two boards together to make a bookshelf. I was following the directions, which said to apply force during drying. Problem is, my directions slipped between the two boards. The glue worked, and now we have an extra-thick board in the garage reliving old dreams of how it was once going to hold copies of the great works of various authors. The do-it-yourself books are in the closet scratching their shiny covers in wonderment that they couldn't even get me past project number one—creating a shelf to put them on. May they suffer in silence.

With the onset of fall and the approaching birth of our

fourth child, my wife has lots of plans. One is for the light in the dining room to be fixed, so we won't eat in the dark for the next five months. I'd just as soon eat at 3:30 in the afternoon as fix that lamp. Electricity scares me. My brother once convinced me to lick the end of a large battery when I was just a kid. Since then, I barely trust light switches, let alone wire. That's what I do: let 'em alone.

You see, I know that even if I walk out to the pole in the backyard and disconnect the whole house, there will be one little jolt of electricity lingering somewhere to get me. I'm too smart for that, and besides, candlelight keeps the romance in marriage and the leftovers in the murky darkness, where they belong.

I recently put a new heating element in the hot water heater. Until then, we could only have enough hot water for half a shower, half a load of laundry, bathing half a kid, and so forth. I spent three hours trying to drain the hot water heater, decided it must not have much water in it, removed the element, and flooded the laundry room. Later that evening, a friend asked me if I had remembered to release the pressure before trying to drain the heater. Some friend! Doesn't he know the damage he does to my ego with questions like that? I fixed the dryer recently, too. It was either that or string a new clothesline. Last time I strung a new clothesline, I thought it was pretty tight. By the time my wife hung out the clothes, it hung so low even the underwear was dragging. She's thrilled I fixed the dryer. All I did was scoot it out, hit it hard with my *Reader's Digest* book, scoot it back, and somehow it works. Hey, I'm a genius. What can I say?

I'm pretty handy with words, too. Like last Saturday. My wife and I were going out to dinner. I sat downstairs while she spent the better part of an hour applying makeup, styling her hair, and choosing her clothes. As she came down the stairs with a Christie Brinkley smile on her face, all I could say was, "Boy, you've really gotten big lately." Not a good choice of words, even if she is eight months pregnant.

For those of you who are handy with your hands, or for those of you with husbands who are, life must get pretty boring. You fix things instead of throwing them away. You refinish instead of replace. You don't eat in the dark or take cold showers. How nice. You can find your tools because you want to. I prefer mine lost, thank you.

20 Glad to Be Getting the Drearies

The drearies are upon us again. That's fall—the season. I know there's lots of wonderful things going on, like leaves changing color, squirrels gathering nuts, bears hibernating, Ma and Pa settling down for long winter's naps. Still, it's gray and wet, and life seems so heavy in the fall.

It's the season we always seem so close to doom and destruction, even as we prepare for Thanksgiving and Christmas. Somehow, summer wars seem like games, compared to the wars of fall and winter. Television films of soldiers being interviewed with backgrounds of blue skies and banana trees look like games, compared to the celluloid images of the same men in muddied fatigues guarding a barricade on a drizzly day in late October.

In the fall, children barely waken from their naps in time to see the sun go down. The sun makes short daily appearances and is even then often shrouded under gray clouds and drizzle.

Do I seem to be complaining? Well, I *did* start out by saying the drearies are here. Actually, the man of the house has a cold, which is not all that big a deal to the woman of the house, who has three little men of the house to take care of already and a fourth one expected to arrive in only a few weeks. Perhaps he will be a little light in the dreary dark.

Anyway, the lady of the house, who used to pamper the man of the house, now hands him a box of tissues on her way to save the day somewhere and reminds him the garage door is stuck open and winter's coming on, just like last year when the garage door was stuck open and winter came on, lingered long, and finally went away. I sneezed, she said "Bless you," and I wished someone would.

We've been busy lately coordinating travel schedules, most importantly the arrival of the cherub himself, or herself. (The "her" is a little hard to imagine, but at this point, God only knows, and He's nice enough not to tell.)

The lady in our house, who seems always to be a mother-to-be, has decided the baby must come the week of Thanksgiving so my mother-in-law can cook the turkey, clean up the mess, get the house in shape, and put up a Christmas tree before she retreats to the safety of Texas. I think a three week in-law visit would be great, and have prepared a short list of other things for my mother-in-law to accomplish while she is here: potty train Donovan, the two-year-old. We've considered selling the home to afford two babies in diapers, but we already took out a second lien to buy ear infection prescriptions and don't stand to clear much.

Ah yes, fall. It does make one think of the happier things in life. Like television. I turned it off just before eight, just after a commercial showed a man with mental powers setting houses on fire. My five-year-old came away repeating the words of the announcer: "Rated R, Rated R, Rated R." The commercial came on right after his favorite show about the Duke boys, which isn't really harmless because it makes

Zachary think policemen are dumb and elected leaders inept. So I turned it all off.

I'm not a total television hater, however. Can you imagine the joy of parents and children reunited after the television shows about missing children? And will those with children ever forget *Adam?* I also know television fills many spaces in the lives of many lonely people.

I'm glad to be getting the drearies so early this year. They're like a cold: You get them once and they help you build some immunities, some optimism. I think I caught them Monday when I drove past a school yard and the water was a couple of inches deep under the swing set. The cutest kids I'd ever seen were lined up at a classroom window with their noses pressed to the glass. As it slowly fogged over from their warm breathing, I just knew they had the drearies, and that's where I caught them.

Just like a cold—wouldn't you know I'd catch it from a kid?

21 In a Children's World

When I was a little boy in about the first grade, I knew very little about the world in which I lived. One of the very first memories I still cling to is of the funeral of President John F. Kennedy. I knew nothing of his presidency, nothing of the Cuban missile crisis, the Cold War, the beginnings of the arms race. Nothing. And I was happy to know nothing.

Things I did know were that I had to get burr haircuts every other Saturday and the gum the barber gave out was the sweetest in the world. I also knew that while my father had gone away, my mother loved me, and that meant the world was all okay. I knew what nights "Walt Disney" would be on TV, that the worst catastrophe on Saturday mornings was the possibility Popeye might not get his spinach on time and the second-worst catastrophe was that my mother might serve it to me. I didn't know what a *nuke* was. A *freeze* meant Mother would cover the plants outside, not that bombs wouldn't be built.

Now I have little boys. And if I allowed them the run of the television, like many parents do these days, they would have had a choice Monday night of watching a special about the president of my early memory or the destruction of Kansas in a horrifying nuclear holocaust my young mind couldn't have imagined, awake or asleep in the deepest nightmare. It is a different world in which my children live, as it was a different world in which all generations became who they became. The generation that created me also created nuclear warfare.

My three sons are so small and soft, though boys they be. They play ferociously all day, getting sweaty and dirty, breaking things, crying, screaming that they did not really cry, losing things and finding them, hiding things, sneaking snacks from the pantry, pushing and fighting, apologizing, standing in the corner, resisting rest, climbing, wanting a finger kissed when hurt, screaming furiously against kisses when there is no pain to vanquish. They are children in a children's world, and I ache sometimes with a desire for them to stay there.

Last night, after their baths, they ran into the living room all steamy and pink. They're still so small all three fit in the tub together. Drops lingered on their faces and in the corners of their eyes and glistened in the wrinkles of all three smiles. I was in my easy chair, and they had come to show me their muscles.

Striking the familiar pose, arms curled and shoulders tensed, hips jutted out, they seriously waited my appraisal. I declared them to have the strength of ten ordinary men. Actually, the little bulges on their arms looked like perfect pillows for a flea, a fly, and a mouse. They're not men; they're boys. And little ones at that.

I know now that when you become a parent you look at the events of life through your own eyes and through a separate visual aspect—the view your children might see if they were not protected by innocence and trust. You think about how events affect you today plus how they will affect your children tomorrow. A bomb in Lawrence, Kansas, for example, means death to us all in Oklahoma. But more than that, it means the end to untold millions of children's dreams, a combined end to what could have been fascinating journeys for our future generations.

You'll never find me chained to a fence protesting nuclear arms. I know that the main reason the Russians don't use theirs is because we have ours, just as well as I know that the main reason we used ours against Japan is because they didn't have them. We live in a strange world where the ability to destroy ourselves becomes an ironic form of protection.

Just as my sons did not know JFK, but will only know him through answering questions about him on a history quiz, I hope and pray that is as close as they will come to nuclear destruction. History is full of horror, just as it is full of hope. History is full of pain, just as it is full of purpose.

I believe as long as men can look at sons and see themselves, then hope and purpose will win out and history will not end. And that is something to think about and be thankful for.

22 Don't You Dears Know What Causes This?

I've known for many months that November would come this year, just as it has every year since I can remember. It generally comes at the same time every year with the same events, like Thanksgiving and the tenth week of the early Christmas sales, which begin as soon as the bathing suit clearances end.

This year, we're expecting a little more than just a turkey on the table. Somewhere very close to Thanksgiving Day, our fourth little turkey is scheduled to make his/her appearance. We've been accused of going to an awful lot of trouble just to be able to skip the annual family reunion.

Seriously, with the baby due soon—this month, instead of somewhere in the future—I've been unable to avoid the usual conversations expectant parents find themselves engaged in between breaths. In the supermarket, at church, with friends and strangers, the conversation piece becomes the protrusion of the once slender, beautiful wife. The tone varies from "My dear, how could you ever let him do that to you again?" to "How blessed you are to be given another lovely child to raise. You must be thrilled."

Somehow, Lisa always manages to look thrilled. Truth is, her back hurts a lot, her hair won't curl right anymore, her skin breaks out occasionally, and she has—at last count—3,875 things to do "before the baby comes." I find myself hoping he (or she) will come tomorrow so we can write the 3,875 things off as a lost cause. Anyone who already has three children knows they can survive without 90 percent of the necessities, anyway.

Having a fourth child brings statements we haven't heard much before. Here's some of them, analyzed:

- *"I guess you're hoping for a little girl this time?"* This one comes from grandmothers holding lovely little granddaughters. The implication is that little boys are nice, "but ahhh, look what I've got." Truth is, we would like to have a little girl. Greater truth is three boys are great and four would be even greater. Guess we can't lose either way. But, if it is a girl, Lisa has more than 4,000 things to do to change the nursery to pink. We'll also have lots of clothes to buy, as gift giving tends to dwindle after the second child, the implication being that anyone with the gall to have four can either afford to clothe them or is too preoccupied to do so.
- *"Just as long as it's healthy, right?"* Right. Only one of ours has had a slight health problem at birth, and we are thankful for that. But then again, what is health when you're talking babies? With the money we've spent on eardrops, baby aspirin, thermometers, humidifiers, cotton, Band-Aids, teething gel, and diaper rash cream, we could have bought a condominium in Colorado, or at least outfitted all the boys in Jordache and Izod for this fall. But, we are lucky. Our boys hardly ever go to the doctor, and we're lining up investors for later trips to the dentist.
- *"Don't you dears know what causes this?"* This statement is always said in a stage whisper in front of an appropriate audience. We politely turn red. Yes, we do know, but we don't exactly know what to do about it, we reply. Then the person who made the statement politely turns red and changes the subject. Actually, we explain that what causes "it" is love. We wanted the baby, and we will soon have it—for a lifetime. That takes a lot of love and an understanding that he

(or she) wasn't *caused,* but *created.* There's a big difference.

• *"This is the last one, isn't it?"* This usually comes from a friend who is a practitioner of the philosophy of "tubes tied after two." We've talked about that. Birth is so beautiful and amazing, we kind of hate to close that chapter of our lives. Children are so wonderful and nice to have around, we hate to say "no more." I know there's an awful lot of kids. I know the world has an awful lot of problems. I've heard all the arguments against big families, and now, I'm happy to be in a situation to argue in their favor in the future. I'm lonely when it isn't loud. I get depressed in crowds of less than four. See, you adapt.

I know the event is near, because the mother-to-be has gone from blooming to mushrooming. She's waiting for me to open heavy doors and asking me more often if I love her—usually after she looks in the mirror. I do. She looks beautiful to me.

23 Do You Hear What I Hear?

"Daddy, you're not listening."

"Sure I am."

"Then I can do it?"

"Do what?"

"See, you're not."

"Not what?"

"Daddy!"

Now that you have been privy to a private conversation of mine, you know I am not the perfect father you thought I was. (You didn't? Just as well, I guess.) Actually, there's no such thing as the perfect father, but then again, there are no perfect children, either. Thank goodness. We wouldn't be able to stand each other.

Back to the conversation above. I put down my newspaper and asked him what it was he wanted to do. Turns out he wants to build a fort upstairs in his bedroom. I told him to go to it. I'm delighted when the boys want to build a fort or anything else, since I have never been able to build anything.

Even after giving up on wood shop in junior high, I was the joke of the leather class. My belts with personalized names made everyone think they had double vision. My wallet wouldn't fold. I couldn't even make my mother a coin purse. I kept telling my wife these hands weren't made for labor. Even garbage bags get the best of me. Every one I've ever tried to carry out has split, so I just don't do that anymore.

I went back to my paper.

"Zachary hitted me."

"Okay."

"It hurted, and I cried."

I put down the paper to see what was the matter. He was bawling on the floor.

"What's wrong?"

"Zachary said I was an Indian, and he hitted me with an arrow. I already told you that."

"You did?"

I can't believe I have neglected two boys in just a couple of minutes. Quickly I told Russell about the victories of the Indians over General Custer and that he could go take a pretend bow and arrow and get revenge.

"Don't let Zachary Custer argue with you, because it's history," I said. And then, I went back to my paper and Erma Bombeck. Columnists love to read other columnists.

"Dirty."

"Huh?"

"Change my diaper. I dirty."

There are times when not listening is neglectful, and there are times when it is necessary for self-preservation. This was one of the latter. I've always had a rough time with those fathers who can plunk a kid down in the middle of a Sunday school picnic, whip off a dirty diaper, and put on a fresh one just as if they were changing the oil in the car. Confession time: I'm not very good at either of those things, but I'll take the oil any day.

"Daddy, I'm dirty!"

"Where's Mommy?"

"She was sweepy—takey nap."

"Me, too." Snore.

"Waahhh. Waill!"

About this time, the no longer "sweepy" lady of the house enters, stomach first—that constant reminder that one romantic evening we decided three boys is not enough. Now that we've had almost nine months to think about that, that evening has lost its romantic glow. (Not really, Mom.) Actually we can't wait for the new baby. We've already purchased him a ticket to Dallas on the first flight after birth, and from there to San Antonio. (Not really, again. Because of nature's perfect feeding system, *el bambino* must be accompanied by the mother of the house, and she's not leaving me here alone with all of them!)

Speaking of them and her, they all walked in together. "Mommy made me tear down my fort!"

"Did you say he could build a fort in his room?"

"Zachary hitted me again!"

"Can't you see that Donovan's dirty?"

"Change my diaper."

"Help," I said.

"They're your boys," she answered. "Remember, 'Like father, like son.' Well, it has a rather truthful ring to it. Now, I'm going to take a nap."

This might have been another good time not to listen, but I had no choice, I decided. If I don't listen to them today, they might not hear me tomorrow.

"Come here, guys," I said. And just think, next week there may be four of them.

24 I Wonder at My Wondering

I have been to countries on the far side of the globe. I have seen the sea. I have flown in the skies. I have ridden the great amusement rides and walked through the dark and dangerous alleys of large cities under midnight moons. I have had victories.

Like other men, I have been thrilled by the events that change our lives. The second ride on the roller coaster doesn't make the heart pound so grandly. No later visit to the sea compares with the first sight of waves crashing on the white sands.

And then there's Patrick. A thrill, to be sure. A pink and squalling miniature mess of slightly wrinkled skin, pinched-shut eyes, matted hair. His legs twisted in strange directions like anyone's would be if they emerged from cramped quarters, as he did. His spidery hands went immediately to his mouth, which was open, breathing life's fresh air, which was returned from surprised lungs in sharp cries. Finally, he was born. A thrill—no less a thrill than the birth of Zachary, Russell, or Donovan before. No less a joy to behold, a treasure to hold, a precious story to be told. Another son, himself to grow and do his own telling, but for now dependent on me to begin his story with a strong opening chapter on which he can create a plot. Wouldn't you know I'd characterize my new son as a book?

I wondered, a few weeks back when we expected Patrick, if I could really get excited about a new son. Now I wonder at my wondering. And, I wonder at much more. So soon after his birth, men died in Lebanon and around the world. Other fathers' sons gave their lives as my son received his. Children starved that day, and cried in streets, cold and naked, as my Patrick was wrapped by a tender nurse and placed in a warm crib for safekeeping.

It occurred to me also that the first thing we want to know about our offspring is their sex. Heavens, this will give them trouble the rest of their lives. Next, we want to know their weight. That, too, will give him trouble, unless he is luckier than I and is one of those perpetually slim people—you know, the kind who doesn't really have any friends.

The next question people always ask is whether he has any hair. I know one thing: I'd rather come into the world bald than go out that way. For me, it's too early to tell.

Then, everyone wants to know if we're disappointed we didn't have a girl. That depends on who asks. If the guy with four daughters asks, I weep on his shoulder. If anyone else asks, I tell them all about my "fantastic four." No, I am not disappointed.

I wasn't sure a few weeks ago what I'd say in my column when the baby—Patrick—came. Turns out, he was delivered about the same time I usually write my column. Kids have a great sense of timing. I had planned to write about the thrill of being the first to touch him, of "catching" him, under the careful tutelage of the doctor, of cutting the cord and claiming him, of handing him to his mother, who had had him all along and didn't need to claim him now.

I'm not going to write about all that. It was the thrill of a lifetime and ties for first, second, and third, and fourth place with the other thrills of a lifetime that bound up the staircase, jump from the coffee table to the beanbags, refuse to eat green beans, and occasionally wake up screaming in the night about monsters in the closet.

I'm going home now, to hold Patrick. First, I will have to hold Zachary and Russell and Donovan. And, I'll hold them as tight and as long as I can. For I know that someday they may walk the dark and dangerous alleys under midnight moons, sail the seas, fly the skies, or visit faraway countries where I will not be with them. Even Patrick, who cannot manage yet to raise his head, has a thrilling story to be told.

I can't wait!

25 And I Know the Hippo Can't Skate

It's got to snow this weekend, preferably mixed with sleet. If it doesn't, the lady who lends me quarters for newspapers and spends my dollars on diapers is going to drag me to a sidewalk sale at the mall and the five-year-old, who trounces me at computer games and has plans to marry half the kindergarten, is running away. Sleet or sun won't make a difference for the other three, for they still need forty-eight diaper changes and eighteen trips to the potty.

Even as I write, Zachary packs his things. Just the essentials: his Play-Doh Fun Factory; crayons for writing home; two red bandanas for covering the face in bank holdups; the hippopotamus he couldn't sleep without; the list of presents he wants for his birthday next month (he expects to find someone generous); one of those disappearing-milk baby bottles (hippos have to eat, you know).

If I were smart enough to sell tickets in advance, I could have made a fortune on a morning like this. People who have already raised their children would pay money for the nostalgic trip, to see us suffer from a safe distance. People contemplating children would buy tickets the way people flock to horror movies in 3-D. Wrestling fans would have paid to see Russell's reaction when he discovered Zach had packed the Play-Doh into his backpack. Shirley Temple fans could have relived her glory days with Donovan's rendition of the orphan when he discovered two-year-olds are too young to run away.

He's heading out the door, and still the sky refuses to drop even one tiny flake. Those of us who aren't really crying are pretending deep sorrow, especially six-week-old Patrick, who has already learned you fight for every inch of attention you can get around here. It is a poignant scene: Mother with two children wrapped around her legs, baby in her arms; little boy waving a tender good-bye as he departs

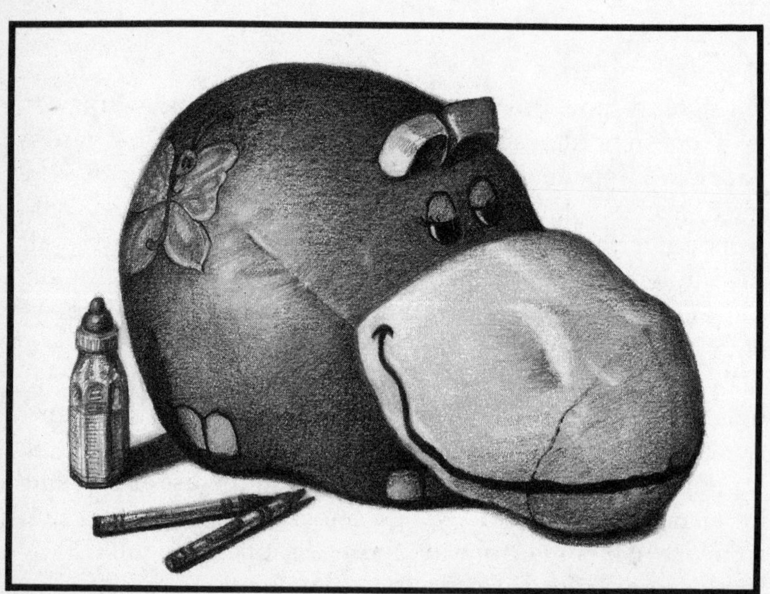

into the overcast twenty degree morning; Father trying to finish his cinnamon roll and praying for snow real soon.

He departs. We scramble to windows on all sides of the house, both floors, trying to keep an eye on him. I told him it was okay to run away, as long as he doesn't cross any streets. He agreed, but that was not that comforting—the only other route leads through a field of cows down to the frozen river. I know his hippo can't skate.

Meanwhile, the other responsible party—my wife—is fixing her hair and applying her makeup in preparation for the demolition derby—the mall sidewalk sale. Mothers must have a special kind of memory that erases memories of the bargain hunting and remembers only the bargain. All afternoon she'll be comparing quality and I'll be chasing quantity; she'll be choosing fashions and I'll be calming passions of anger; she'll be choosing and I'll be losing little boys by the dozens.

It still isn't snowing, but Zachary returns. He couldn't get in the tree house with his mittens on, and his hippo got heavy. The tribe gathers around my typewriter to play with the Play-Doh. Patrick sleeps and Mommy primps. I watch the clouds.

When I said "I do" seven years ago, I had no idea what I was going to do, and now look what I've done. I'll feel personally responsible for overpopulating the state if it ever happens, while at the same time, the stockholders of Carter's, Pampers, St. Joseph's Chewables, and Tide can thank me for their huge dividends. I know four children—even four boys—is not exceptional. I get letters from people who've survived all this and are thankful for old age. They tell me silence is golden because you don't notice it again until you're fifty.

I have a friend who's thinking of settling down soon, having a couple of kids. I'm three years younger and have twice as many as he ever intends to have. Somedays he sleeps till noon, he's never seen "The Dukes of Hazzard," stepped on a plastic dinosaur at 4:00 A.M. on the way to a crying baby, or forgotten to kiss his special girl for several days when juvenile demands were extra heavy. In a few years, he'll know how good that kissing can be when you finally get to it.

"Are we all ready?" she asks, in a voice that sounds expensive.

"Sorry, dear," I reply. "It's started to snow. How about a game of Candyland?"

26 A Lady of Capacity

We arrived at church at the same time and parked in the same lot. A quick smile, a short wave, a notice of the morning's brisk breezes made bearable by the sunshine, and then we both tended to the business of getting children out of the car.

Seat belts had to be undone and children lifted from the car for the weekly inspection before going inside where everyone is supposed to look their best, act their best, and emerge even better than when they went in. Another sunny Sunday.

It is only when I arrive at the lot at the same time as the woman and her daughter that I remember again how many times people said, "Well, the main thing is, he's all right," every time we presented the world with another bouncing baby boy. I always agreed, but wondered really, what does "all right" mean, and how do you really know?

I remember an aunt saying, when she heard we were pregnant for the fourth time, that God was giving us all these children because we had so much love, such a capacity to care. I told her that might be true, but carelessness had at least as much to do with it as caring. She turned a pleasant red and seemed to enjoy it. She doesn't often feel the pleasure of embarrassment.

And then there's the lady in the lot. Or, rather, the ladies, for her child is not a child anymore, but a woman like her mother. They are the best of friends. That is obvious from only the few times I have seen them together. I can imagine them sitting in the sun on a back porch, snapping beans, if people do that anymore, listening to music, reading to each other from favorite books, discussing the morning sermon, planning dinner.

They have spent the daughter's life together, though I don't know how many years that may have been, so poor am I at guessing age. The mother, though, has aged. She has the worn look of someone really loved, like a teddy that never leaves a child's side until the child no longer needs it and puts it under the bed.

It is this woman who has the capacity for caring my aunt talks of. Perhaps that is why she has a daughter who cannot walk, and I have three sons who can and a fourth who probably will. It is she who lifts a daughter weighing probably as much as she does into a wheelchair and asks only if she is comfortable, while I, at the same time, fuss over my sons' slowness at climbing out of the car on the tough little legs that save me heavy loads.

I imagine God looks over each child He sends into the world and considers carefully where he or she should go. And one day, looking at a beautiful baby girl with auburn hair and a great capacity for love, He looked hard to find the mother who could return that love and brush that auburn hair for the little girl whose arms might not have the strength or coordination, but whose eyes want to see a reflection of pleasure, like all little girls'. He looked for a parent who would rather spend a lifetime lifting the growing child into wheelchairs to go places than stay at home pitying the child and herself for where they might have gone.

He looked at the child and then He found the parent, a little woman with a massive heart and a tremendous spirit. A lady of capacity.

I know I'm not out of the woods yet. We live in a world which, for all it boasts of being civilized, has more ways to maim and cripple than ever before. There are still diseases and disasters. There are still activities and accidents, and, as they say, "Boys will be boys."

So, on that sunny Sunday, playing baseball in the yard with three boys chasing, laughing, falling down, learning to use their muscles with coordination, pushing their little bodies to do more and more, I sought more love. I can stand on the pitching mound and envision them as perfect runners for the race before them. As a father, I find them easy to love. The newest one dozed in a baby swing. I already picture him stumbling with his first steps, drawing his first pictures, saying his first words.

Maybe I have a capacity for quantity. That takes love, too. Still, it's comforting to know there are people willing to carry children all their lives and not just walk beside them. I wonder if I could?

27 The House's Revenge

We put our house on the market today and began looking for a new one. You may be familiar with our old one. If "Ripley's Believe It or Not" or "That's Incredible" knew about it, they might send out a film crew immediately. The nightly news might be interested in doing a film feature on the potential buyers and their reactions following tours.

I can see the promos: "Young Couple Seeks Divorce After Visiting Hunter Home. Film at 10:00 P.M." The newspaper headlines might read: "Realtors March for Birth Control" and "City Council Considers Banning Crayons in Residential Areas."

Really, it's not all that bad. It's just sort of "lived in." You know, the kind of older home everyone is looking for? Especially the director of the latest gothic thriller, *The House's Revenge.* The realtors have had little trouble finding interested buyers. Lon Chaney, Boris Karloff, and Vincent Price (or their ghosts) have been by. They say Bette Davis may drop in. There's even talk it could be converted into a memorial to Alfred Hitchcock.

Our house may be declared a momument to historical motherhood. It would not be the first honor our lovely home has received: It's already been declared a monument to *hysterical* motherhood. Our area could use the tourist trade, and rather than fixing up the place, the realtors could allow the children a little more freedom to increase the market value for the tourism industry.

Just in case you are unfamiliar with our house, I'll take you on a brief tour. But, do be careful—a quarter of a billion in accident insurance is not really sufficient for the dangers which await our guests.

The Front Yard

There weren't any stickers when we moved here. We imported them from Texas, imbedded in eight tennis shoes, pants cuffs, and so forth. There were flowers, but they were all picked last spring when the cat died. The driveway had many more rocks, but they were transported one by one to the sandbox in the backyard. The sand was removed to the trunk of the car, accidentally left open after groceries were unloaded. The trail you see by the sidewalk represents childish independence and a refusal to walk on anything intended to be walked on. Let's go inside.

The Living Room

This room is "lived in." Ignore the carpet, and it will ignore you. Otherwise, look out, because it has a mean personality. I'm sure you could get a new screen for the sliding door. Russell ran through it when Zach was chasing him. It was about five degrees below zero, but luckily the glass door was open—you know kids. The carpet is a most unique feature of this gracious home. Called "early and late Kool-Aid," it combines spills and splats to their best advantage and is color coordinated with the drapes, which were created by jelly hands on white and change design each time a visitor arrives during breakfast. For no additional cost, we will remove any semblance of furniture.

Dining Room and Kitchen

Julia Child and the Galloping Gourmet would consider this place their greatest challenge to culinary creativity. She would be speechless. He would be kept galloping, as is Lisa when she prepares meals with four boys underfoot. You may glance in the refrigerator, but please do not open anything in Tupperware. That's the only culture we have around here, though it's definitely growing. The oven is new, but please don't ask why. The garbage disposal works—you'd be amazed how well—as it's been well fed. The dining room floor is concrete because it hoses off better than carpet and tile and wears well under Hot Wheels.

The Stairway

This is where we measure our children. The grease stains and grime marks on the white paint indicate they are growing rapidly. Watch for toys, especially marbles and plastic dinosaurs with ribbed backs. It's a bit like running a mine field, but *if* we make it up the stairs, you'll love the boys' bedrooms. Wait, where are you going? You haven't even seen the view of the backyard from the upstairs. Hmm. Must be out of your price range.

28 Guess Who Got a Faulty Fairy?

A full four days after Zachary lost his first tooth, the tooth fairy still had not made a visit, even though I had assured the little grinner that the fairy always comes, even when the tooth is lost, like Zachary's was. Guess we got a faulty fairy, I explained guiltily.

And then I found out how much brothers—even little bitty ones—care about one another. There have been times when I doubted any of the boys other than Zach would reach age four with limbs and hair intact. I've seen a two-year-old body screaming and flailing as it fell out the back patio screen door. I've heard screams worthy of the best late-night TV followed by, "I didn't do nothin' " in an innocent but defensive tone.

One night I heard one of the boys praying that God would take away Russell, just like that—whoosh! Off in the night! Sometimes I think I've been blessed with four kids who were all misplaced, originally intended to be only children in different households. They call one another buddy and declare "may the best buddy win."

Then, this morning, Zach came down with two quarters and announced that the tooth fairy had finally come and paid his dues. He elaborately told his little brothers how the fairy apologized for being slow and gave the extra quarter and promised never to miss another tooth in the Hunter family. That could be twenty-odd trips a year, at least. Another crisis had been averted, as the boys put out of their minds the fears they had built up that the Easter Bunny had run away with the fairy and might very well keep Santa from his appointed rounds as well. Once again, all was right with the world.

Only one thing: I didn't put those quarters there, and neither did the fairer fairy of the house. It was the five-year-old fairy, Zach himself, with money out of his bank.

I heard him plotting the whole thing, spelling it out to Patrick, who at ten weeks old is a pretty good confidant. "Patrick," he said, "see these quarters? They're gonna be from the tooth fairy. And when I wake up in the morning, I'm gonna show Russell and Donnie, and then they'll know the Easter Bunny'll come."

And then he whispered, "Patrick. There's no fairy, but it's okay."

Later that night I looked under his pillow, and the quarters were there. At breakfast the next morning, he put on an act better than any parent I've ever known, and I could have shot myself for falling asleep three nights in a row without putting a quarter under his pillow.

It reminded me of a story my pastor told, which he had read and you may have heard before. It's a good one:

Johnny was told that his sister had a dreadful disease that he had had and conquered a couple of years before. He was just a little boy, but he understood how bad it was and was very sorry for his sister.

When the doctor told Johnny his sister needed a transfusion and that he was the best person to give her one because their blood matched and he had already had the disease, Johnny's lip quivered as only a little boy's can. He hesitated as he thought about his sister and finally said, "For my sister? Sure."

The day came for the transfusion. The little girl lay pale on her bed. Johnny was in the bed next to her, healthy and robust. As the doctor inserted the needle in his arm, he turned and looked at his sister and smiled a comforting smile. She smiled back weakly, and the blood began to flow from his arm to hers.

As the transfusion was completed, Johnny looked at the doctor, one small tear sneaking out of the corner of one eye, and asked, "Doctor, when am I going to die?" It was only then that the doctor realized why Johnny had hesitated. When he said "Sure," he thought he was being asked to give his life for his sister.

The story of the tooth fairy is not in the same dramatic league, and what Zach did was no big sacrifice. It still told me that brothers love one another and as a father, that's one of the best pieces of news I can imagine.

The next morning Zach came down the stairs with two more quarters and the biggest grin he's worn lately.

"Hey, Dad," he said. "There really *is* a tooth fairy. Look!"

"I know," I answered. "I saw him as he left last night. He said he was sorry it took him so long, but he thought you'd understand."

29 Through the Fog of Exhaustion

We passed a milestone this week as parents. It happened in the midst of cold pizza, melting candles, helium-filled balloons, and an off-key song. There was lots of laughter, a big mess on the floor, and our "baby" was suddenly six.

Lots of things in life don't last, like plastic swimming pools, New Year's resolutions, typewriter ribbons, living room furniture, spring, sunsets, fireworks displays, banana splits, vacations, income tax refunds, and babies.

Some things last forever, like visits from relatives, potholes, toothaches, winter, rainy days, carrot salads, potty training, bank notes, car payments, and—I'm told—teenagers. I'd take a cracked plastic swimming pool over a permanent potty chair any day.

When you're holding a tiny baby at two in the morning, trying to keep yourself from falling out of the rocking chair, using mind over matter to convince yourself your feet aren't frozen to the floor and your eyes aren't puffing to the point of permanent disfigurement, you can't imagine ever having a six-year-old. Instead, through the fog of exhaustion, you imagine other things—like bachelorhood. You remember back to everything from college to kindergarten. You pinch yourself to keep awake long enough to know for sure he's asleep this time. As you lay him softly in bed, you notice the sun rising cheerfully outside his nursery window. Twenty minutes in the shower does nothing to convince you this child will ever grow up. And then, suddenly he's six.

Of course, he has brothers who are three, two, and new. The parent still rocks children at sunrise, but also wakes one up on the way to the shower and drops him off at school. Diaper by diaper, day by day, and then suddenly there's mountains of little white underwear where the box of Pampers used to be.

I'd like to have back the time I wasted thinking of the time I was wasting holding a kid who wanted nothing more than to be held. Little Donovan always says "up there" and points at me, and I realize how big I must seem to him and how far "up" must be. Sometimes I say I'm busy, but the best times are when I lift him up and we seem to him to be somewhere far removed from his little world on the ground. Only a short time ago, he was just a little rug-hugger, mixing saliva with carpet dust as he pulled himself around. Now he's doing laps around the yard on ten-inch legs, punishing me with his astonishing growth.

One of these bright mornings, Patrick will turn over with no one's help and, being astonished at his power over the world, begin exerting a natural force toward independence. In the blink of an eye, arms that cradle becomes arms that stretch out to catch stumbling new walkers. In another blink they are limited to catching fleeting hugs on the run or pulling up covers over dreaming little bodies gathering strength for a new day of conquering.

If I had a dollar for every time an older parent has told me how fast my children will grow up, I could retire and enjoy watching them grow. I've joked about whether they were comforting me or warning me, but I know. It hit me in the middle of a birthday party, with a slice of pizza in midair, sitting at a table where I outweighed most of those present four to one. They were chattering in little-boy voices about which planet in the solar system is the biggest. Was it Saturn? Was it Jupiter? They couldn't agree, but they knew it wasn't Earth.

The reason it hit me then was that I remember taking a two-year-old outside on a warm summer night and pointing at the darkened sky and trying to explain the moon. I remember he thought it was so big, "the biggest thing in the world." And now his world's changed and the moon's forgotten because he's so big. I decided right then that I still have to work at being his father—their father—or I'll just be the moon, and not the biggest planet in their solar sytem, and "up there" will be somewhere else, instead of where I am.

30 Wiping Away the Gripies

I bet you've never tried to diaper a butterfly. I haven't, either, but three-year-old Russell has, and his inability to do so was one of his biggest Monday disappointments. All the bears had diapers, as well as the giraffe, but the butterfly was bare.

Santa Claus brought him the silk stuffed butterfly last Christmas. Russell is forever singing, "If I were a butterfly, I'd thank You, God, for giving me wings." Being earthbound, his great goal in life was to befriend a butterfly. You know how Santa cooperates on goals like those, so the other boys have bears, and Russell has a butterfly. (He'll love that story when he's seventeen and invites his girl over for dinner.)

I wonder sometimes about teaching boys to care about beautiful things. Why do some boys like busting things and some like Beethoven, and why do so few like both? Why does Russell like butterflies and Zachary boa constrictors? Russell's no sissy, as any parent who ever tried to corner him in a play-devastated living room will attest.

And then there's tears. Russell has the biggest tears in the world. We've considered moving to Utah and restoring greenery to the desert or inventing eyeglasses with built-in dams and reservoirs. He calls them "gripies," and wants them wiped away, not so much because he is embarrassed, but because he fears drowning.

Zachary, on the other hand, screams and growls instead of shedding tears. His tear ducts must be in his throat somewhere, lending energy and volume instead of salt. It's not so

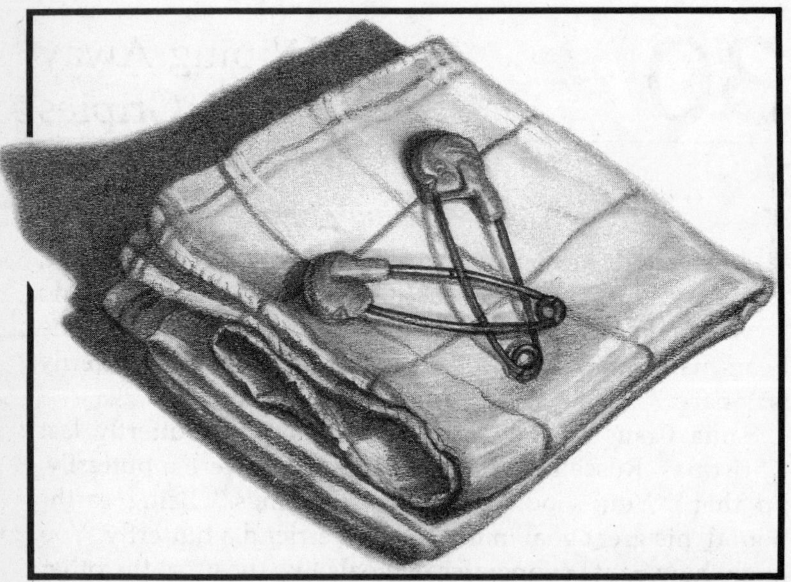

much that big boys don't cry; it's just more effective to imitate earthquakes. Good thing we live in the country.

I remember feeling a little relief each time a baby was born around our house, because all four of them turned out to be boys. I thought, "Well, I know all about boys. I can raise them guys." Yeah. Right. Only I didn't realize that while both waterfalls and whirlpools have a lot in common, they don't work the same. Of course, they're both dangerous, which is something I learned really quick about boys, too.

What do they have in common? Well, neither of them can remember to flush the toilet or put down the lid. Neither of them is all that brave, unless the other one is around, and then he's twice as brave as the other one. Neither one of them will eat a good supper unless there's a good dessert waiting. Neither of them likes any of his toys until the other one does. Neither of them likes their younger brothers unless one of the older brothers picks on them.

Both of them care about beautiful things. They care about either bears or butterflies, and both are beautiful. They care about each other, and little boys are beautiful. They don't care much for little girls, unless the little girls look like little boys, which some do, and that in a way is beautiful, too. They'd care about sunsets if baths didn't follow so closely. They'd care about Beethoven if it were the background for a "Scooby-Doo" cartoon.

They do care; it's just that caring has to be defined on their terms and not mine.

They don't give a hoot about politics, for which I'm thankful. I could not stand arguing ecology with butterfly Russell or the right to protest with a screaming Zachary. Right now, I'm the president, the congress and the supreme court all rolled into one, and they do care about that. Come to think about it, they do care about me, and that is beautiful, too.

Now I really must go. I have this handkerchief, which I

normally use to wipe gripies. I just happened to think it might fit this young winged friend of Russell's.

31 Anybody Seen My Cool?

Saturday morning I helped him clean his room. Sunday afternoon we tossed a Frisbee on the front lawn. Monday morning I yelled at him and drove him twelve miles to school in total silence. I lost my cool, and I can't find it anywhere.

It all had something to do with blue jeans that wouldn't button, a belt misplaced, and tennis shoes soaked from treks in mud puddles. It may even have had something to do with the fact it was his next-to-the-last day of kindergarten. Next-to-the-lasts always have a certain amount of pressure. Besides all that, his hair absolutely would not comb, the breakfast-cereal box did not have a prize inside, and somebody put the ice cube trays back in the freezer with only about one-third of the cube slots filled with water. To quote a literary legend: "It was a terrible, horrible, no good, very bad day."

All day long I looked for my cool. It wasn't at the office. It wasn't in the car. (Just ask the lady who pulled out in front of me at the red light.) I walked down Main Street and saw my reflection in the windows. Yep, my cool was definitely misplaced. I thought it might be at the park, but there were only squirrels and unmowed grass. No cool. I crossed a beautiful bridge on the way home in the afternoon, and I looked over the edge. Cool, blue water, but not *my* cool.

I searched the yard at home. I remember I had felt pretty cool the day I built the tree house, but standing under it had no effect today. My new riding mower didn't make me feel cool at all. My cool was not in the garden, not in the garage, not in the garbage, not here, not there, not anywhere. "Woe is me," I wailed. Only two weeks after turning thirty, I'm forever uncool.

I couldn't find it inside the house. I looked in the back of my sock drawer. I looked on top of the refrigerator. I looked in the bill file. I looked behind the encyclopedias. I looked everywhere that I normally leave things. No cool.

In a room-to-room search, I finally ended up in Zachary's room. I remembered how Saturday we had cleaned it together—how he had put puzzles together while I made the bed, picked up blue jeans and muscle shirts and stiff socks, straightened a closet Indiana Jones would run from, and sifted through nine months of kindergarten papers with the number five printed backwards by my only left-hander.

Sitting there alone on the foot of the bed, unconsciously holding Potbelly and Beaner Bear, I surveyed the room for damage. Amazing what forty-eight hours can do to a squeaky-clean room. In the middle of the floor was a train set and a car racing set cleverly arranged so that no trains can cross without colliding with a car or two. An exaggerated rubber tarantula hung from the ceiling. A complete zoo of stuffed animals was piled on the bed. Two dozen hats, most of them memories of Grandpa, hung over the headboard.

Posters adorned the walls. There's Roger "the Rolaid Cowboy" Staubach, the crew from "M * A * S * H *," Kermit the Frog, the University of Texas tower lighted in orange, a Pontiac Trans Am, Olympic athletes, the presidents of the United States. On his desk were baseball cards, model cars, everything from Care Bears to G.I. Joe. It was a complicated room for a complicated kid. I was struck by how so much of what was in the room had become unfamiliar to me. I thought of how as he grew, I tended to visit him in his room less often. I want him to see me as part of the world he carefully builds around him, so he can find me here when he needs me—just like he can always find Kermit or Hawkeye Pierce.

While I was in thought, he entered.

"Hello, Zach," I said carefully. "I was just sitting here looking at all these cool people on your walls and wondering who you want to be like when you grow up."

"Oh, you know," he said, looking me straight in the eye. "You."

I couldn't help but smile with relief. Here I'd spent the day looking for my cool, and he'd had it with him at school, keeping it safe for me. I'm just glad he didn't lose it.

32 Keepers of Secrets . . .

We were surrounded. Everywhere we turned, hungry eyes peered forth from the darkness with menacing looks. There was no escape, as each end of the table was blocked by a body leaning backwards with two feet of the chair off the ground. Directly across was a threatening urchin in a high chair. An even smaller, but just as disruptive, being wailed from a playpen in the corner.

It was dinnertime, and the troops were less than pleased. Candlelight can't hide leftovers from kids who can see ghosts in the dark and gorillas in the backyard. "What do we get for a snack if we eat this stuff?" They may be young, but they know the value of making a good deal in advance. This time, however, all four went to bed hungry, because there wasn't anything to bargain for. The cupboard was bare.

My kids can stand a little starving. Lisa will make up for it when she hits the grocery store tomorrow and the national economy takes an upswing. President Reagan may take credit for it, but the truth is, my children are just getting older and we're consumers a colony of King Kongs couldn't match. So they went to bed hungry. I've been told that dreams are better on an empty stomach.

I watched them sleep—a hobby of mine. I tried to imagine other children sleeping in fear, their senses ready to shriek them awake, their tummies shrunken from hunger, their bones weak or perhaps broken, their hair matted from uncleanliness, their clothing old and torn, their skin scarred from burns or discolored from bruises. They, too, dream and occasionally cry out. They don't cry out often, though, for they fear the ones who might respond.

They are the children of the sick. They are the victims of child abuse. They are loved by people who don't understand love. And they are legion. They may be the little girl in your Sunday school class, the boy who throws stones at your mailbox and runs, the youngster who peeks from the window across the street, the little blonde who laughs too easily and cries too often at school and sometimes doesn't know which to do. The abused child may be your nephew or your boss's daughter. She could be your grandchild or your own child. It may have been you. It may have been me. Both the abuser and the abused are keepers of secrets.

As my little boys twist and turn under covers, feet poking out, hair sticking up, I wonder about their dreams. Some they'll embellish in the morning and others will slip way inside, never to be remembered but forever a part of the boy. Some they may turn into reality and others they may run from. But at least they do dream.

Last year, twenty-one beautiful children died in our state, stabbed, beaten, drowned, smothered, shot. With them died their dreams. No more flipping around on soft sheets and fluffy pillows. No more make-believe in sandboxes or underneath card tables. No more anything, just cold, dark reality.

I'm not saying all this just to depress you, for I believe, as Carl Sandburg said, that "Children are God's opinion that the world should go on." I just wish I could assure the world would go on for all those children whose crime it was to laugh and play loudly and friskily, to tease and question, to want to dream without fear.

I had an "accident-prone" friend in the fourth grade who was always bandaged and occasionally sporting a new cast for us to sign. He cried in the rest room at school, but he always smiled when he walked down the hallway. We teased him for his clumsiness and never chose him for our teams because he was different somehow. I was just a little boy; I didn't know the secrets he kept, or the dreams he may have dreamed, or how many came true.

So when I look at the four blond heads poking from covers, I hope they're dreaming. I hope they'll never encounter nonaccidental pain or be abused for trusting. I remember asking about the little tombstones with hearts and lambs in the cemetery after I attended my grandmother's funeral when I was very young. Someone told me that all the little children probably died of pneumonia some cold and rainy winter. I believed her.

I'll teach my children to come in from the cold and to look both ways before crossing the street, but it won't be enough if I don't teach them about diseases of the heart and mind. Maybe together, we can all help the other children and keep their dreams alive.

33 Mother Was a Two-arm Pincher

I know the comeback that long, sculptured nails is having has been hard on kids, especially in church. When I was seven, my mother could look so peaceful and reverent as she kept her full attention on the sermon while digging craters in my bare defenseless arms with the longest, prettiest, strongest, bright red fingernails. For every peep out of me, there was a pinch out of her.

In fact, my mother was a two-arm pincher. She could sit me on the right and my sister on the left and keep us in line without ever taking her eyes off the pulpit. I just knew someday after I had grown up and didn't sit with her anymore she would absentmindedly pinch some kid beside her, who would howl out loud and bleed from unconditioned arms. I guess I was lucky, though, because I had a friend whose father was a construction worker and would grip the top of his leg when he acted up. Poor Jim always limped out of church. He couldn't sit still, and he couldn't walk straight.

Sunday night, one of mine got completely away. I had missed the beginning of the sermon because he had said, with his usual lack of timidity, right during the prayer, "I need to go."

"What do you mean?"

"You know—*go!*"

"Oh!"

So we went. He waved on the way out and he waved on the way back, and I tried to tell myself that the older generation in the congregation was overwhelmed by his cuteness and charm, if not amused by the color of my face.

We'd been back a couple of minutes when I looked at his chair and found it empty. Now this was a new situation. This particular kid had snored in church before, laughed uncontrollably, fallen off his chair several times, drawn pictures of the preacher in a hymnal, and thrown a paper airplane made from the bulletin, but this piece of magic was a new maneuver. He had vanished, and since the rest of the congregation was still present, I felt safe in assuming he left under his own power.

Then I saw a clue. A shoe—an empty shoe. An empty Velcro Wildcat tennis shoe, two rows up and just to the left. *What if my son is stripping under the pews somewhere?* I mused. The amusement was not to last.

I heard some stirring under the chair he was supposed to be in, and realized he had returned. "I lost my shoe," he said. "I want my shoe," he threatened to cry. "I'm going to find my shoe."

My wife's fingernails are too short to be of help, and she happened to be in the nursery with another son and about ten of his peers. I don't have the hands of a construction worker and no vise grip handy. Where is my mother when I really need her?

I was lucky today. I gave him my best "One more move and you're on your way to the moon" looks and he slumped down in the chair as if he had craters in both arms and vise grips on both knees. He hardly breathed till the final amen.

Someone asked me one time if I thought I would be able

to love four kids and if I really thought it was right to bring that many boys into a world like this one. You betcha, on both counts. I love all four of them, and bringing them into the world is the best way I know to make sure the world stays at least as good as it is, if they'll just grow up to be the kind of men we need to keep things spinning.

I forgot to tell Russell I was upset by his behavior. Nobody else mentioned it, either, to me or to him. I bet there were some men there that night who would have liked to have been able to unlace their brown wingtips and set themselves free. Maybe even some of the ladies would have liked to slip out of their stylish loafers and get comfortable for the worship hour. Not to be sacrilegious, of course, just a little less pious.

It's awfully hard to be patient with your own children. When other parents flee from the sanctuary with a kicking kid, I smile and say, "Kids will be kids." Not my mother, of course; she's busy sharpening her fingernails and remembering Sundays past.

34 Robby Romper's Rubber Room Restaurant

I've been thinking lately about putting in a restaurant. You see, like most of the Pepsi-pizza generation, we eat out a lot, and with four children, it tends to be the raw adventure of it that keeps us going back for more.

Parents of young children approach restaurants much the same as mountain climbers survey the jagged peak and sky divers check their gear before taking the big plunge. Choosing the peak, choosing the landing spot, and choosing the restaurant are one and the same. All three experiences are challenging and exhausting. Each requires physical fitness and dedication to the sport.

Surviving the experience of taking four young boys out to eat depends on preparation—getting enough rest beforehand, mapping out strategy, mapping out routes to the rest room, learning the tolerance level of certain eating places—and skill. The pizza-generation parent has to know when a look is enough, when a snapping of the fingers might do the trick, when the urchin's offense is worthy of a kick under the table or a very public trip to the rest room (which you try to find a table near). However, a kick under the table is dangerous when the kickee's legs are only fourteen inches long. At worst, you'll kick the chair instead of the kid. At best, he'll fall howling out of his booster seat.

With all this vast experience, I think I'm ready to open my own place. I'm going to call it Robby Romper's Rubber Room Restaurant. I'm going to do the fast-food places one better by going to rubber fixtures instead of the popular all plastic look prevalent today. Even the floors will be rubber, so kids can fall all they want. We'll have the Catsup Room, all in bright red, to match the menu's main condiment. Other family dining rooms include the ever-popular Pepperoni Palace, the much in demand Hot Dog Haven, the ultrachic Luigi's Grilled Cheese, and for tough little chicos and chicas, the Belly-up Burrito Bar.

All of the rooms will be soundproof for the convenience of the temperamental child or impatient parent. Catsup and mustard won't ever be served in a squeezable container, and Parmesan cheese will come in throwaway containers to guard against two-year-olds who like to lick the top when no one is watching. (Eaten pizza out lately? Got a cold?)

Every forty-five seconds, the chairs at the table will rotate, saving you the hassle of moving the children away from whomever they have been sitting by for the past forty-five seconds. In the rest rooms, you will be able to watch instead of work: the sinks will be low, the water won't turn off automatically after three and one-half seconds, the potties will be near the ground. The hand dryers will be positioned to dry hands, not children's hair.

There will be nothing to ride on, nothing to watch on a big screen, no one walking around in funny costumes. While the menu is limited, the food will taste good. It has to, without all the above-mentioned distractions to make you forget you came to eat. You will pay your bill with tokens instead of money, as this convinces the kids they had a good time.

No tipping will be allowed. However, you will be required to hose down your dining area after you eat—that's why everything's rubber. On the way out, every child will receive a free T-shirt to put on immediately to cover the stains. Every mother receives a box of Biz; every father a packet of fizz—Alka Seltzer.

Depending on your experience, you're welcome back, or welcome to stay. After all, the rooms are rubber. Nothing could be finer, than to bring your minor, to eat out in my diner. I bet I'd be a success!

35 Growling When I Should Grin

Wouldn't life be simple if our kids always did exactly what we asked them? There would never be dirty socks posing as a bookmark in the wedding album when old friends come by. There would never be tennis shoes at the bottom of the swimming pool or a full roll of toilet paper half-flushed. There would be no chocolate stains on the curtains, no half-eaten Pop Tarts under the couch cushions, no frogs in the closets or turtles in the bathtubs.

We could cut a cake that didn't have fingerprint trails across the icing, scrub in a tub that didn't have rings worthy of "Ripley's Believe It or Not," have broccoli for supper. Wouldn't life be simple? Wouldn't it be grand? Wouldn't it be boring?

The fact that there is sand down inside the window on the driver's side of the family Suburban is irritating, I grant you, but it means the kids are active and healthy, loading up the sand, hauling it around to the front, and cramming it down the window, all without notice. They didn't tell on one another. They said something about a dust storm with real big dust. Maybe if they can learn cooperation through mischief, they'll be able to accomplish some good things together, too.

If they were always obedient, I could find a tie tack to wear to church. But then I'd discover that tie tacks are out of style right now and I'd look like a drip, so I guess they're saving me embarrassment. I could make it to the pantry without tripping on the mountain of crumbs on the kitchen floor from the cookies that were supposed to be saved for the reception at church. In fact, if they always did what I told them to, I might get to eat a cookie myself sometime.

Wouldn't parenting be easy if we always knew what to expect? We would only cook when we knew they would eat. We would always be ready when they came with a hurt. We would always have the answers and the advice.

There's another side to all this: Wouldn't being a kid be easy if you knew what to expect from your parents? Wouldn't life be simple for our kids if we were as consistent as we are always sighing for them to be?

Just think, we'd never break promises or make promises we know we probably won't keep. We'd never get irritated and angry over something we thought was so cute just twenty-four hours earlier. We'd never say yes when we meant no, or no when we meant yes. We'd never nod behind the evening paper and then come crashing down on a three-foot kid who did something he thought he had permission to do.

We'd never hold a two-year-old close and call him our sweet little baby and then later tell him in a rough voice to quit acting like a baby. We wouldn't sit in a chair and worry about the late car payment, the rising electric bills, and the lawn that needs mowing while pretending we're really irritated about the Hot Wheels car we stepped on at the bottom of the stairway or the "M*A*S*H*" poster that got shot up before it could be hung up.

There'd be no gamble in crying, because the kids would know in advance whether we'd still put them in the corner or sweep them off their feet and into our laps to cry together. They'd know whether or not to beg, because they'd know in advance whether we were serious about "no surprises this trip" or if we're flexible enough to spare a buck or two. They'd be able to look into our eyes and see tiredness and worry and plan their hasty retreats.

Isn't inconsistency fun? It's the adventurous part of being a family. I honestly don't always know what to expect from the boys, and they can't always count on the expected response from me, either. I have growled when I should have grinned. I have tickled when I should have paddled. I have probably hurt when I should have hugged.

For their part, they have told stories when I needed truth. They have covered their ears when they needed to listen. They have remained quiet when they should have talked.

We all say things we don't mean and mean things we never say. We jig when we should jag, go left when right was better, back when we need to push forward. Luckily, this means we are always running into one another, bouncing off, and having the fun of inconsistency. Life is never simple—and rarely boring.

36 Opting for Option Three

"Look at all the children who have grown up," I said. "Why just the other day I was at the grocery store line behind five other shoppers, and not one of them had a box of diapers or package of teething biscuits in the cart. It wasn't a dream, man. It was reality."

Here I am again, talking to myself. How can anyone with four sons feed their Hot Wheels habits—not to mention helping them avoid ice cream withdrawal—and still afford counseling? So I talk to myself. But no one knows. All parents do that, anyway.

I was standing on the porch. Russell was on top of the car with a heavy metal dump truck loaded with rocks. Donovan was standing on the bumper, ready to "receive the load," which soon knocked him flat on his back behind the car—in the mud. The temperature was over 100 degrees and it hadn't rained in days, but there was a mud puddle. And there was Zachary, holding the water hose.

My instructions had been clear when I let them out the front door. "Stay away from the car. It's been waxed. Keep the water hose in the grass. And please, *please,* be nice to each other." Some people have Cabbage Patch Dolls. I have cotton-ball kids: Their ears are permanently stuffed.

"All right, guy," I told myself. "You have three options. You can scream so loud they stand in frozen shock until you knock all three to the ground like a screaming bolt of lightning. It might work, because they don't think you can move that fast. Or, you could go quietly inside, pack your bags, call a travel agent, and book a single one-way ticket to the closed city of Gorki in the Soviet Union. Or, there's always option three: Pretend you never saw, go back in the house, and ask the wife if she has checked on the kids lately. Then sit in the chair by the window and watch the action." Fathers who enjoy sports on a Saturday afternoon always opt for this option. It's amazing what a 5′4″, 120-pound female middle linebacker can do when provoked by the other "team."

I like a counselor who provides viable options, so I quietly close the door and look for Lisa.

"Hi, dear," I say. "Wonder what the kids are up to? I've got to fix a leaky faucet or something. Mind checking?"

With a sly smile, I slide into the chair by the window to watch the fireworks. She opens the door, stands poised on the porch, and surveys the action, unseen by the trio of tiny tenors whose voices fill the air with threats, tearful cries, laughs, and warnings not to tell Mom. I couldn't wait to see how she would handle it. I fairly shook with glee at my ability to free myself from this one parental pressure point. My counselor told me how proud he (I) was.

Nothing happened. I noticed she was coming back in, and I scampered to the kitchen to find a faucet—hopefully a leaky one.

"Hi, sweetheart," she said sweetly. "I just remembered I haven't set out a thing for lunch and it's time to nurse the baby, too. I just don't have a spare minute to check on the boys. I do have a feeling they're out front. Would you mind? You can fix the faucet later."

At this point, who could I turn to? I was down to two options, neither appealing. I didn't feel like a bolt of lightning. I didn't want to go to Russia. I didn't want to spank kids, either, but—and here's a confession—I do. (And I did.)

You know, they say that a husband and a wife begin to look like each other after they have been married a few years. I don't know if that's true or not, but I know this: We seem to be seeing the same counselor.

37 It's a Good Word

I wasn't spanked much as a kid, though I do remember my mother laying a yardstick across the back of my legs when I was about eight. I took the yardstick away and broke it. That was the end of spankings for me, although Mother, whose memory never fails, may have a different story.

Anyway, the opportunity—well, actually, the screaming necessity—to spank my six-year-old arose the other day, and I tried to make an objective decision. I had read the reports on children's punishment in my wife's magazines.

I even remember that "Dear Abby" said it is okay to spank a child until he passes the sixth year. I know where my wife stands on the issue, but then, the opportunity—or necessity—arises much more often for her. She's home all day with the famed quartet of miniature machos who make church nursery workers tremble and close friends forego birthday parties for their little Johnnies and Susans.

Past advice aside, it was all between me and him. Normally, I like to think things through, but I committed myself rather quickly by throwing out one of those dangerous parental words: *"If . . ."* So, when he stood there with his feet planted firmly and tore up the picture he was holding in his hands, I found myself facing a second dilemma. If I didn't spank him now, would he ever trust me regarding discipline again?

I spanked him, the psychological benefits of which I won't get into here. If you can't decide when or if to spank your children, write Abby, Ann, or my mother.

The next day was Saturday. My wife was gone for the day and I was alone with three of the boys, so I decided to keep an eye out for that word (*if*). Here's my report, verbatim.

- *"If* you don't want to wait until I get downstairs, you can just fix your own breakfast."
- *"If* you had toasted the bread before you put the jelly on it, it would have worked better. And who said you could have chocolate syrup on your corn flakes?"
- *"If* you cannot quit kicking your brother under the table, then you may leave the table."
- *"If* you were so hungry, you should have eaten your breakfast. Now, go play outside."
- *"If* you ever come through that door with muddy shoes like that again, I'll turn you over to your mother."
- *"If* you ask one more time when your mother is going to be home, I'm putting you in the flower bed to pull weeds."
- *"If* you didn't know which ones were weeds, why didn't you ask? Your mother will kill us both."
- *"If* you were so hungry, you should have eaten your lunch. Now, go play—inside."
- *"If* this room is not clean before your mother gets home, I'll take a torch to all your toys."
- *"If* you ask me one more time when your mother will be home, you will do without supper, young man."
- *"If* you don't like what I have fixed for supper, you

don't have to eat it. And quit staring at it. I followed the directions carefully."

- "*If* you were so hungry, you should have eaten your supper. However, since I wholeheartedly agree, here's some crackers and a banana. Now, go to sleep."
- "*If* you boys don't turn out the light, I'm coming upstairs and tucking you in like you've never been tucked before."

When this last *if* elicited no response, I pondered again the ultimate *if*, the threat of a solid spanking. I dragged myself up the stairs and rounded the corner into the bedroom where I had allowed all three to sleep in the oldest's double bed.

"*If* you three aren't . . . the most beautiful little guys I have ever seen," I said to myself. No one else was listening. There they lay, one clutching a blanket, another a bear, and one barely there. Only a few golden curls and a limp hand hanging off the side of the bed represented the youngest of the three.

If. That's a good word, if used properly. For instance, what if I didn't have those boys? or their mother? Now, *if* she would just hurry up and get home.

38 We're Still a Couple

To be a good parent, there has to be a whole lot more in your life than just your kids. I've always believed that, maintaining that if you get all wrapped up in just your kids, someday you might just be the wrapping paper around an empty box. They do grow up.

So why do I feel like brightly colored cellophane with Muppet imprints? Why do I feel like there's a bow in my hair? Why do I feel like I belong on the shelf at the Hallmark store? And why is it as hectic as holidays around here every day?

It's pretty bad when the woman of my dreams hears the man of hers (me) say upon arrival at a posh resort, "Oh, the boys would love those fountains. I wish we had brought . . . oops." What I mean is, "Aren't those romantic, with all the color. Kind of reminds me of Russell's favorite bedtime story. Oops again."

At first I thought it was just me. Then, when we went into a souvenir store, she kept saying, "Now, don't touch. We don't want to have to pay for something we don't want."

"Yes, Mommy," I said. We could have wept if the words hadn't sounded so natural when accompanied by a nearby crash. Someone who had brought in a three-year-old had just purchased a crystal unicorn that now had no horn.

On our vacation, we played shuffleboard, Ping-Pong, Pac

Man, miniature golf, tetherball, pinball, pool. We went bowling and swimming and sat up yawning and laughing over Trivial Pursuit. Quite accidentally, but quite often, we would remind each other how much the boys would love all this playing we were doing. Even when we ate out, we ate pizza, hamburgers, tacos—menus only a mommy could love and dinners only a daddy could dig into with consistency. We've been ordering off the children's menu for so long, we didn't even notice they serve things like prime rib, lobster, and quiche these days. We had thought that went out with our wedding.

"That little boy is about Donovan's age," she said as a three-foot green-eyed bolt of energy flew into the wading pool with his mother's towel and *Redbook* magazine, laughing on the way in and then crying when his nose filled with water.

"That happens all the time to Russell," Lisa said to the lady, who was mourning how she would never know what

Lady Di's chances are of having twins, as her *Redbook* sank to the bottom of the pool. "He's really cute," she said to the lady, who watched the gleeful one carry her tanning lotion and sunglasses off towards the deep end of the grown-up pool. "Does he know how to swim already?"

About the last day of our vacation, after we had found out that the baby-sitter had taken the boys to the zoo, to a picnic in the park, and swimming at a friend's house, we began to relax. We noticed the sun still sets with gorgeous color over lakesides; that cheesecake by room service might as well be cherries jubilee in a Paris cafe; that her hand is still smaller than mine and softer, despite thousands of squeezed mops and scrubbed dishes; that we both still have blue eyes, and that we don't have to tell jokes to laugh with each other.

It's not important to know that I won just about all the games we played, though I throw it in here for accuracy's sake. It's not even important to say we argued a little; it just takes a while to unwind. It's not even important that we didn't call every day to check on the kids—we just forgot.

What is important to me, and perhaps to a lot of couples who think they may have permanently become "threeples," "quadruples," or worse, is that we found we're still a couple. Just like the night of our honeymoon—when I was on the balcony of a high-rise watching the lights of San Antonio go out, wondering if she would *ever* come out of the bathroom—I spent a lot of time thinking. All the time she was in the bathroom.

I remembered that, long before we were parents, even before we were a couple, we were friends. Then I realized that we still are; we just have a larger circle of much shorter friends.

Know how we ended our vacation? We took the money we had left over and spent the afternoon in a toy store, picking up a few things for some good friends of ours. All right, guys, let's play!

39 The Best Year of His Life

The best year of his life is not that far from being over. He doesn't even seem to be aware of the waiting world as he sits in innocence on the kitchen floor, one tooth on top and one on bottom, contemplating a bug that made its way into the house when the door was left open. He's not even old enough to know that edible items shouldn't move when you reach out for them.

He can't walk, and he can't talk. He doesn't have to bear any responsibility for his bodily functions. He is never expected to be patient or considerate, to make or keep promises, to ask permission or forgiveness, to put anything away. He's not even required to play.

Patrick's just a lump in the bed a good bit of the time, just a little bottom under a yellow blanket and a fuzzy head against a crib pad. Just a soft breath, barely audible when the air conditioning cuts off. Just a cry in the night that means hunger and not fear, because he doesn't know of nightmares yet. Just a plump little lump.

Actually, we call him Goobatrick. Maybe it is because of the originality my mother displayed when she named her children Mike, Deb, Thom, and Sue, but for some reason, I have to have names *and* nicknames for our boys. So, we have Zachary, Russell, Donovan, and Patrick, who answer better to Z-Beck, Roosie-Goose, Bodark, and Goobatrick.

We have pets, too. Two dogs, named Back Sunshine and Down Brown Dog. And we have fish, named Hungry Fish. The dogs bark at strangers and the fish entertain children, so even they have a job to do. Everybody does, except Patrick.

Once we learn to walk, we have to get things for ourselves, and then for others. Once we learn to talk, we can get in trouble for what we say, and we have to answer when we do something wrong. Too soon, we learn to hit and we learn to hurt, we squash bugs in an attempt to destroy, rather than in a misguided attempt to fight off our hunger.

The other three lumps on a log—Patrick's older brothers—are helping him achieve a more mature status as quickly as possible. They taught him how to climb the stairs, but not how to climb down. He developed his own method: leap and learn. They've about taught him to swim, by filling the bathtub to their chest level, about two inches above Patrick's nose.

I know why God doesn't give us good enough memories to remember being babies. Who wants to remember the day a three-year-old was proving he could do somersaults and you ended up under his sneakers during the victory dance? Who wants to remember falling asleep in a high chair while your mother did the dishes and bathed the children and you crusted over with Gerber egg noodles, vegetables, and potted meat?

I'm sure we'd all just as soon forget the day we first bit through the nipple on a bottle of apple juice, unaware of what teeth were really for. Who cares about the day our older brother sat us on a tricycle, tied our feet to the pedals, and pushed us down the curving driveway? I don't remember dirty diapers, soggy T-shirts from teething, spitting up, rolling off the couch into a Tinkertoy castle, spilling banana pudding in my lap, getting kissed all over, and having people blow bubbles on my belly.

If I could really remember all those things, I wouldn't dare write about them.

I looked at Patrick the other day in his car seat, head pitched back, eyes closed, mouth open. He was asleep as only babies sleep, who know there is absolutely nothing in the world that could wake or harm them. His face glistened with the sticky covering of his first-ever Tootsie Roll Pop. Even his eyebrows were sugary and red. He had drooled the sweet juice until his shirt was pale pink and the wetness had spread almost to his bare feet.

I studied him a minute because I knew he would soon be plucked out, perhaps screaming, scrubbed clean, "wrapped in squalling clothes," and put away for the night. He couldn't care less, really, for he's enjoying one of the best years of his life—one he'll never remember.

40 Remove the Day and Claim the Peace

Dear Boys,

I'm sorry I got in so late last night. I know you must have moaned when Mommy told you I had a meeting. I think that was your third word, Russell—"Momma," "Dadda" and "meeting." I thought of you when I listened to a speech tonight, more than I thought of what the speaker said. I decided you were probably busily dumping sand into the air conditioner compressors or washing the car with mud—summer fun.

Later, during questions and answers, I pictured all four of you in the bathtub, crowded like oily sardines and almost as smelly, trying to figure out how to get Mr. T down the drain so Luke Duke can rescue him and Mommy can try to melt plastic figurines with Drano tomorrow. I know the room looks like a miniature version of a posh men's athletic club as you stand lined up, pink, steamy, and naked, for a rub-down by the rub-weary masseuse-Momma.

About the time I went to the car to begin the drive home, I knew you were climbing the stairs for bed, searching for E.T., Beaner Bear, Potbelly, and the yellow blankie. I can almost hear the threats from your mother and the promises from your brothers. The promises will be broken and the threats forgotten before another dawn begins.

Tonight you were tucked in, not thrown in bed. You were kissed on the cheek, not tickled in the tummy. Your hair was brushed, not tossed. You fell asleep as your mother rocked the smallest of you, guarding the night against any of you who would dare set a toe beside the bed and threaten the peace she was compelling. Eventually you gave up and all the breathing settled into a rhythm—a quiet chorus of deception.

Yes, she has her gentle ways. And I have mine. I climbed the stairs quietly, counting the creaks, watching for booby traps or possibly even bodies, remembering the time Donovan tried to come down for a late-night snack and fell asleep halfway down the steps, perilously perched in peaceful slumber. I stood at the top of the stairs and looked into both rooms, alternating my gloating gaze. The future sleepeth.

Russell and Donnie were molded together in the middle of the bed they share, surrounded by assorted and sundry stuffed beings whose status changes daily. Potbelly, the hippo, had his nose stuck into the corner of the room, and I wondered wearily what he had done wrong tonight. *Will that hippo ever learn?* I asked silently as I granted him pardon and piled him in the bed with the other fellows. I kissed you boys good night, stood back, and wondered if there were really any better place in all the world than your untidy room and jumbled bed.

Across the hall, a face peeked out from under covers and mumbled a child's dreamy hello, making little sense but all the difference in a weary day approaching end. Only one eye opened, the other smashed into the pillow; only half a smile could be seen, as the rest of the mouth rested on a bear who has no hair.

I kissed you, too, Zach. Three hours earlier you would have resisted, but now you would have been offended by a pat on the head. After all, you're a firstborn son, not a puppy. Now Patrick, sleeping rump high in the crib across the room—he looks like a puppy: ears sticking out, drool making puddles on the mattress, teeth marks in his toys. He gets a peck on the back of the head, where it's safe and dry.

Before I enter my own room to remove the day and claim the peace of night, I pause with a hand on the stairway light and notice it is not on. The rooms are lit by the moon, which makes you boys seem even softer in your slumber, in contrast to your childish energy in the sunlight. You're a soft glow that turns to a mighty roar in daylight.

Life includes many meetings, and you guys know that. You'll have them yourselves someday, and I will wait in my bed to hear your tires, your keys, your creaks on the stairs, and the gentle closing of your bedroom doors. It'll bring back memories of when I turned out the last light at night.

But for now, guys, just remember what you did today. I don't have a meeting tomorrow, and I want to hear all about it. Meet me by the stairway.

Love,
Dad

41 Wishing for the Sounds of Silence

The refrigerator started making a funny noise this morning. I was sitting there eating my cold cereal when it (the refrigerator) sort of fluttered, making a noise like a fan with a bent blade. I savored the cereal. It may be the last bowl of cold cereal for a while.

I was reading in the living room last night when I heard a sound across the room. It was a loose screen rattling against the patio door. When I started up the stairs later to go to bed, I noticed the bottom step creaks. A few minutes later, lying in bed, I listened to the steady drip of the faucets in the bathroom sink and bathtub.

I turned over on my side and the mattress creaked; after eight years, it's wearing out. The last thing I heard as I drifted into silent sleep was the sound of the garage door crashing closed at the far end of the house, all by itself. *It's not supposed to do that,* I thought as I drifted into quietness.

Fifteen minutes later, I awoke to someone else's nightmare and about killed myself at the top of the stairs, trying to figure out which bedroom the moans were coming from. It's Zachary, and the nightmare's over, but across the hall, one is dying of thirst and the other is drowning in a puddle. Meantime, the baby, Patrick, who seems to sense the slightest movement in the middle of the night, is awake and hungry.

"Hey, guys, let's party," I want to say, but don't.

So why is it housewives and mothers don't feel bad when they scan the classifieds looking for a maid or a baby-sitter or someone to do the ironing, yet a father or husband feels guilty about even thinking about hiring a handyman to fix the patio door, straighten the garage door out, replace a board in the stairway, or fix the plumbing? If we don't get a few things fixed around here, I'm buying earplugs.

I grew up in apartment buildings. If something broke, you called the manager. If he didn't fix it, you called the landlord and he fixed the manager. It was all so simple. You paid half your wages in rent, as well as a massive deposit you knew you'd never get back. You dreamed of someday owning a home . . . where you could piddle around with little improvements . . . to give your little honey her dream house . . . to raise your one little boy and one little girl . . . and then retire someday . . . reading *Reader's Digest* in a hammock under two broad-leafed maple trees. What a life!

What a laugh. I've got a manager (me) who's allergic to tools and a landlord (my wife) who thinks the answers to all life's questions come in a can of WD-40. The tenant-landlord-manager all-in-one arrangement results in a "spray-and-see" outlook on life, fixing it, and the pursuit of happiness.

Hiring someone to fix something around the house is perceived by my wife as being the same as hiring someone to play with the kids. After all, I'm not Prince Charles, and we don't exactly live in Buckingham Palace.

Playing with the boys is not always a piece of cake, either. In this one weekend, I was asked to turn a tricycle and an old piece of wood into a go-cart with racing stripes and automatic steering; repair a broken swing; rewire a walkie-talkie; put together a model of the space shuttle Discovery; replace two tubes on a bicycle; paint a Dukes of Hazzard race car; play soccer, baseball, and football. We didn't get around to swimming.

I'm almost as good an athlete as I am a handyman. I have about as much luck with baseball as with broken refrigerators, though the boys aren't old enough to know that the stories of my winning the pennant are a little stretched. I figure our refrigerator is opened about 7,763 times a year, which is about how many times I strike out playing baseball. Of course, if I'd play ball more and open the refrigerator less, the refrigerator, my batting average, and I would all be in better shape.

There may be things I'm not good at, but I want my boys, when they're grown, to remember one thing: I was there to hear the creaks and the moans, and I was there to swing at the ball. That's bound to count for something.

42 Heaven's Got Room for Gigglers

I remember Zachary, my oldest, asking an occasional question about death, usually after finding a squashed frog or seeing the remains of an animal struck by a car. I did my tender best to explain it wouldn't be all that bad when it came and that it would come for all of us, sooner or later, hopefully later. As usual, I talked a lot and said little at the same time.

I won't have to explain it to Russell. Between Dracula and Mrs. Maule, he's got it all figured out. Mrs. Maule is his Sunday school teacher, and she loves to talk about heaven. The Dracula part figures in because one night we left the kids with a baby-sitter who let them watch *Draculu* on TV. Neither life—nor death—has been the same since.

I know Mrs. Maule would never like being in the same sentence with Dracula, but she would be pleased to know her interpretations are winning out. Russell's only four, but he believes solidly in heaven, though he thinks the idea is kind of funny.

Sunday night at church, the pastor preached on heaven, and Russell thought it was so funny he started giggling. His giggle box absolutely flipped over, flowed over, and spilled out into the aisles. He reached full-fledged laughter almost before I wrestled my way out of the sanctuary with him. Actually, it wouldn't have been so bad except, as my younger sister can attest, I'm allergic to laughter in church.

All I have to do is hear a mere slip of a giggle and I'm gone. So Sunday, just when I was about to pinch or poke or pound Russell into solemn attention, I began to giggle myself. Respectable thirty-year-old fathers of four sons do not laugh during church—unless of course the preacher says something funny and wants everyone to laugh. So, on the pretense of taking Russell out to gently prod him into submission, I took him under arm and chuckled toward the exit.

Russell quickly told me he knows church is not heaven, because no one ever gets spanked in heaven—but they do in church. Soon he embarked on his favorite subject and I learned that if you fall out of a swing set in heaven, angels catch you and you never get hurt; you can't get dirty; you never cry; and every time your daddy goes somewhere, he takes you with him.

He says he's not sure where heaven is, but the trip there is not near as long as the drive to Texas.

"You fall into a coffin and then you're dead," he said. (I think that part must have come from the Dracula movie.)

"Your eyes are closed, but it's not dark, ever again," he

went on. (I think that part must have come from Mrs. Maule.)

"Steps come down from the clouds and you just walk right up," he continued. (I don't know where that came from. Probably a life insurance commercial.)

I imagine when I was four I thought only old people died, but Russell knows better. If heaven is a happy place, that means there are lots of children to play with, so Russell decided that children die, too. I could have struggled with the words to tell him that, but he just knows it and says it, and it's okay.

So why would a writer who pens a column about children, which is supposed to be humorous, write about death, which isn't funny under the best of circumstances? Well, if you really write about children, you have to write about death, too. Even though I still have all mine, maybe you don't, and maybe you'll feel better if you can think your child saw heaven the way Russell does. He knows he'd never get in trouble for giggling there.

At night, Russell pulls his covers up to his chin, insists a light be left on and flashlight placed beside his bed. He then wants his mother in the rocking chair until he falls asleep. He's afraid of the dark, but he's not afraid of heaven, because it's never dark there. "Mrs. Maule said so."

43 First-Grade Drop-out

I was positive my kid was going to be so stunning as a student that his teacher was going to call me after his second day and tell me Zachary had restored her faith in the profession and convinced her that low pay, shrinking respect, tired feet, and lousy coffee are all worth the price. His brilliance and creativity would renew her spirit and revolutionize first-grade teaching methods.

So why, on the fourth day of school, was I pulling him through the double doors with a scowl on his face so wide he had to turn sideways to get through? Why had he refused to get on the bus? And who is the kid Zachary has sworn will never live to take his first numbers test?

The first two days of school were great. The second day, he got on that big yellow school bus and disappeared from view with hardly a look back. The third day, he came home from school with a "burn the books" look, a cut behind his ear, a slide burn behind his knee, dirty clothes, two papers marked with happy faces (which he promptly tore into little pieces), and his schoolbag, which he put back into the closet where it had stayed all summer.

First grade was not going well at all.

"I want to be a moron," he wailed. "I'm not going back to school, and you can't make me. Never. Nohow. I hate school." With that, he left the room without saying what was wrong, which left me wondering. What had devastated his dreams of glory on the playground and having his own desk and chair?

Maybe he threw up at lunch. I did that once. I just got nervous and lost my lunch, right back into the tray. No one hardly noticed until the teacher came by and told us we were supposed to clean our plates. I had to explain why I couldn't, and that story haunted me for years. Maybe history repeated itself and Zachary threw up.

Perhaps he split his pants wide open. I did that once, too, and tried to walk backwards all day. If you forget just once, you *really* have a problem. I wanted a drink from the fountain and bent over. It wasn't funny then, and it isn't funny now.

It could have been that the teacher asked him a question he couldn't answer, but I doubt it. Rather than getting upset, he would be more inclined to tell her she had neglected to effectively teach him the answer, and since he cannot yet read, he has been unable to research it for himself. Well, he might not say it exactly that way, but he'd say it.

It couldn't be that he runs funny. That had been a kindergarten problem, and we had worked it out. Now he runs like Carl Lewis. At least he believes he does. It isn't his hair. We had it styled before we bought his school scissors, so he wouldn't cut it himself, like he did last year. It couldn't be he forgot how to tie his shoes and everybody was watching, because he wears Velcro-fastener shoes.

Later that night, I figured out what it was. It was the arch enemy of the first grader: the second grader. Someone just a little bit bigger, a little bit faster, a little bit tougher, and a little bit bossier. Zachary's big, fast, tough, and bossy, but he's also a first grader. So it wasn't the cut behind the ear, where a fist missed but a fingernail didn't. It wasn't really the burn behind the leg from when the second grader "allegedly" pushed a reluctant first grader down the tall slide that kindergarteners weren't allowed on the year before.

It was a broken heart. After all, he had believed only Mr. T or the President of the United States was really bigger than a first grader. I guess I hadn't ever told him there is always another mile on the other side of the milestone. There's always another grade and a bigger kid. So there he is, hurt feelings, surging emotions, crushed spirit, sagging self-worth. Cut down in the prime of life by a seven-year-old who hasn't learned yet about third graders and so runs the roost like a playground pirate, pillaging and plundering the smaller prey.

Well, I've been plundered and I've been pillaged, and it's only a sight better than splitting your pants or losing your lunch, or even running funny. I don't know if I can handle being the parent of a first grader. It's a real jungle out there!

44 Somewhere There Lives a Child

Somewhere there lives a child so loved, so secure, so serene he never fears. He never worries. He never cries at night. He never flattens his nose against a window pane and watches red taillights disappear into a night. He never brushes away tears with the back of his hand or wipes his drippy nose on his shirtsleeve.

This child has never awakened in the dark and trembled. He has never been chased by a bully or cornered by a dog. He never took his first ride on a Tilt-a-Whirl or tumbled from a bicycle. He is so secure he is unsure what pain is or why other children cry.

This child lives in the imagination of those who love children. He is a dream, a coloring book picture with rainbows, toadstools, caterpillars, and little frogs hopping around a little child with a shining face. He is a fantasy—a miniature prince astride a beautiful unicorn, surveying his kingdom where everyone is good and no one ever hurts. Yes, if he lives at all, it must be in our imaginations.

Somewhere there lives another child, loved, but less secure, lacking in serenity, full of fear. He never flattens his nose against the window pane, either. The taillights disappeared long ago, blurred by tears on pillowy cheeks. The shape of the lights has almost disappeared from memory, as have some of the features of the man who drove away.

This child lives in reality. He is the child of divorce.

As the father of four sons and the son of divorced parents, I understand both of these children—the serene and the insecure, the peaceful and the trembling, the happy and the hurt. One is too real and the other is too much a figment, too great a fantasy to be believed in.

Maybe it's the so-called seven-year itch, but there are a number of couples of our acquaintance who have decided recently to throw in the collective towel. Rather than replacing those worn-out wedding gifts, they're dividing them up. Suddenly, it's "This is yours, this is mine" bargain basement days. More homes are being converted back to houses, while little kids sit on the porches with their chins on their knees, watching their beds go into the back of a moving van. Questions are asked; answers are lacking.

We have always said a man's house is his castle, but consider the child. His house is truly his castle, for it is where he has slain the dragons that lurk in the corners. It is where he has wrestled other mighty warriors and won victories for his kingdom. It is where he has rested his weary frame from the battles of the day and the vanquishing of his foes. It is where all subjects bow to his will and there is no fear. It is where he has servants striving to fulfill his needs with the finest in raiment and the most delightful delicacies for the appetite of a growing conquering hero.

I can remember an old house with an attic opening over the hallway leading to the kitchen. I had never really been up there before, but in my daydreams, I had battled many a foe with my daddy at my side. He had never feared the attic and could walk peacefully through the hallway to the kitchen. One night, Mother sent me down the hallway to the kitchen, and I couldn't go. I was scared to walk beneath the attic opening, for my father was gone, and it really was an attic and not the opening to a mysterious magical cave with buried treasure. It was reality, and reality was a scary thing when faced alone.

It is funny (well, not really *funny*) how "society" learned to accept divorce; how psychologists and counselors tell people to "free themselves from binding, loveless marriages." We stand up for our rights, no matter who we wrong.

And a child lives with a permanent vision of slowly shrinking red lights, the insecurity of whether someone will answer his cries in the night, the fear he may have done something wrong, the worry he isn't learning something his daddy should be there to teach him.

If it sounds like I'm just trying to make someone feel guilty, I'm not. I've been the child, and now I'm the father. I just think we need a little less "society" in our castles and a few more answers for the warrior.

45 Sometimes We Break a Heart

It was a hard decision to make. Here was this six-year-old standing in front of me, telling me he can kick a ball higher than any person in the whole wide world—including me. He's my son, and I like to agree with him and build him up. You know—tell him he's the best and all that.

So, what do I do? I kick the ball clear over the house. And we live in a two-story house. A *tall* two-story house. There's no way a six-year-old can kick a ball over that, as is proven by his thirty-six attempts following my success. Suddenly, he is beaten by the one person he was sure would never do that. His shoulders slump, his face runs with dirty sweat from overexertion, his shoes are untied from his kicking, his ball has rolled off under the evergreen bushes to hide. Zachary doesn't want to play anymore. At least not with Dad.

I felt like a traitor as I watched him slink away without congratulating me on my victory. Like every father of sons, I knew he still loved me with the same fear and intensity he always had, as both a confidant and a competitor, as a partner and as public enemy number one.

I'm afraid I'm in for a lot of combat, for that is how it is with fathers and sons. They are bound by history and instinct to grapple with each other, to test their wills, to

"best." Whatever limit I set, my sons will want to push to the limit with a natural rebellion to test my strength and perseverance. Today I can stand in the yard and kick a ball over a two-story house, but I can tell that nature and time are on his side. It's a matter of time and energy, and he has more of both.

I've lost so many games by a point—on purpose—just to make the kids the victors. I can't count the times I dropped a ball to let a boy reach first base or pretended not to notice how long ago strike three was passed. On rainy days, we sit before the computer game and I let the Wumpus devour me to keep the score even. He asks me, "Dad, what's seven plus one?" and I say "Nineteen" so he can say "No, eight," and beam. I pretend not to see him when he sneaks up behind me as I read the paper, and then I fake a heart attack and lie on the floor, frightened to death until he tickles me awake—and I'm not even ticklish.

Every boy wants to believe he has the best father in the world and that he will grow up to be just as good a father as his father is. On the other hand, every father hopes his son will grow up to be a better father than he was. We have a goal of creating the man who betters us, so we prod him and discipline him, challenge him, and make him work beyond himself. Sometimes this means losing to build his confidence, and sometimes it means winning to make him feel the bite of competition and strengthen his emotional determination.

Sometimes, too, we break a heart, but it isn't always our son's. Sometimes we break our own hearts by teaching our sons to stand up for themselves, when we really want to stand up for them. We hand them a shield instead of being one, and we watch, biting our lips and biding our time. Before it is all over and they have grown, we teach them how to lose, because, as every good father knows, losing is part of being successful. Sometimes you kick the ball over the house, and sometimes you wink and miss it, falling on your fanny.

There's this constant struggle for attention: "See me do this. See me do that." Then, when I want to relax, to be left alone, watching a moving story on television, the boys make eighteen trips through the front door, stand on the porch yelling till the windows shake, punching one another out, and coming to me for judgment. If I want to read, they want to hear it out loud and then pronounce it "boring," if it isn't on their level.

I've got four natural-born competitors who know how to defeat any competition for their time with me. But, there is a time when all fathers must surrender the battle and let their sons be victors. I can handle that, for I know they'll all grow up and get their just reward—four sons each.

My gosh! That's sixteen grandsons! But no more balls to kick over the house. Grandfathers aren't competitors.

46 In the Whole Wide World?

I've got news for all young couples who are afraid that when they get married they will have to give up their nightlife—the bright lights and exciting activities of the evening they enjoy together. The news? You give up nothing.

As the sun sets on the horizon, the excitement begins to mount in families all across this broad nation. Mothers and fathers gear up for battle after consulting the *TV Guide* to see what they will miss this evening as they ready their children for an 8:00 P.M. bedtime. If they're lucky, they'll catch the late news, or at least the weather.

Rub a dub dub, four boys in a tub. I can't for the life of me figure out how they can be so thirsty after drinking all that bathwater, yet thirty seconds after they lie down, clean, prayed over, pajamaed, diapered—the works—they're parched for water. Thirty minutes after that, someone is wetting the bed.

Last night, Patrick threw up. Now, I know that's not a pleasant subject, but to the three older boys it represents something akin to a passage into manhood for the baby. You see, it wasn't merely a "spit up"—all babies do that. Last night was a full-fledged upchuck, of the change the clothes and sheets and sponge the mattress variety. While

Patrick was carried to the bathtub, the crowd gathered to discuss the momentous event. Patrick was the instant hero of "Saturday Night Live."

"It's 10:00 P.M. Do you know where your children are?" Not really. Russell's in Zachary's bed, and Zachary's in Donovan's bed. Donovan is draped over the top three steps of the stairway, where he paused to think of a creative reason to come down. One hand holds on to his "blankie" and the other holds on for dear life. His eyes are closed, his breathing even. It's like watching the space shuttle sit silently on a launching pad waiting for the dawn.

Some singles go out to bars to look for conversation on lonely nights. I'm never at a loss for people to talk to. I go into the boys' bedrooms after they are asleep and have some of our best conversations.

"Hey, Russell," I say enthusiastically, "Do you love your daddy? Do you have the best daddy in the whole wide world? And, aren't you the best Russell in the whole wide world?"

He jerks to a sitting position, shows a little-boy smile drunk with sleep, opens his eyes as wide as tomorrow morning's pancakes, and says "Yes." He never wakes up, and tomorrow he won't remember a thing.

In Zach's room, I get a kiss—something he currently thinks he's allergic to. I also get a lot of promises about how good he will be tomorrow and how he won't ever hit his brothers again and will never talk back to his mother or try to turn over the recliner when I'm dozing off. He'll never remember a thing, either.

I don't talk to Donovan because he'll pop right awake and say, "Please turn to channel forty-three and 'The Pink Panther.' Bring me my cereal, please, and turn up the heater." You just don't risk waking up that boy. As for Patrick, he'll initiate his own conversations throughout the night and, until he learns to speak more clearly, I assume he's hollering for Momma.

Spooks are afraid to come into our house because of all the bumps and shrieks in the night as the boys fall out of bed or have nightmares. One good shriek can be followed by three good bumps as feet hit the floor, heading for our bedroom. It's 3:00 A.M. and *now* we know where our children are.

You never know who you'll wake up next to or at exactly what time. I've been awakened by busy committee meetings held three inches from my nose. It's Saturday at 6:00 A.M. and they're trying to decide how many tree houses can be built in a day if we have to wait till after "The Smurfs" are off before we get started. With plaintive eyes they cry in unison, "Promise you won't read a newspaper today."

Our nights are never dull, but our days are dulled by our nights. I was told once by a mother of teenagers to enjoy it now, because the nights get lonely again when the kids grow up. Kids grow up? I thought that was an old wives' tale!

47 A Fair-haired Boy in a Striped Shirt

I sat across the table from Russell this morning and studied him so intently you would think I was trying to count the golden blond hairs on his peanut-shaped head. I watched his mouth curl and uncurl in rhythm to the giggles he always brings to the breakfast table to counterbalance my morning grumbles. I smiled, too, as he licked clean each jelly-covered finger and hopped from his chair to dare the day.

I never look at my children as if it were the last time I would see them, but I was staring intently this morning. Just yesterday, Russell had slipped away for a twenty-minute eternity.

With all his four-year-old gumption, betraying all his teachings, he slipped away in a crowd at a homecoming parade and made his way to Kentucky Fried Chicken for a drink. For twenty minutes of agony, half the parents of our town searched the neighborhood, the school buses, and the ditches for a fair-haired boy in a striped shirt. Even the sheriff issued an APB. But that's what he came down to: "A fair-haired boy in a striped shirt."

For me, he became Adam Walsh. Never had I considered my sons not growing to be tall and strong, handsome and caring—near perfect. And even now, with all back in the fold, I still think no harm could ever come to them. When

he was found, he gave them my name, and life was back to normal.

But then came the meeting of the second boy. He, too, was fair-haired, but about seven. He was a giggler, like Russell. His shoes were untied, his jeans baggy and torn at the knee, but he didn't care, for he had his Hot Wheels and his park, and now he had someone to play with.

All he didn't have was his father and his mother.

"Robbie" came up to me where I sat on the bench watching my four boys.

"Want to go with me to watch them play Frisbee golf?" he asked, pointing across the creek to a group of young men. "My mother said I could do whatever I wanted to do until she got back."

"I have to stay and watch my boys," I answered, and the conversation began. In the next thirty minutes Robbie asked more questions than my four boys put together ask during a Cowboys football game. He wanted to know how old I was, if I liked my sons, if I knew how to fix his Hot Wheels car, if I knew where his mother had gone.

I answered, "Thirty, yes, yes, and no."

He had, shall we say, a colorful way of expressing himself, but toned it down finally after he got to the question, "Do you go to church?" He walked with me and my boys around the park, down by the creek bank, where he jumped in and my boys stood by, dying to do the same but fearful of the ever-present master. He told stories of all the things he's done, only I got the feeling they weren't stories, but the truth of a sad son. And always, he asked questions.

We hadn't intended to stay in the park very long. Our own children were tired and cranky, but Robbie was having a ball. He held tight to the time and did his best to entertain us all, to keep us from leaving him there alone with his broken car. Each time I fixed it, he broke it again and brought it back to me.

Finally, his mother returned for a brief moment to tell him she would be back later. I wanted to talk to her, but she quickly left. Robbie seemed almost not to notice as he pointed to a squirrel and began to sneak across the sandy playground. Slowly, we wiped sand from the knees of our sons and loaded them in the car, and finally I said good-bye to Robbie, who parted with one last question: "When ya' comin' back . . . huh?"

As we drove away, I stared in the rearview mirror and caught sight of Russell, the one I had almost lost, waving good-bye to Robbie, the one I found but couldn't keep. He was driving his Hot Wheels through a drainage pipe, and my mind searched for his father, just as earlier that day my mind had searched for my son. Something is wrong.

48 I Still Need Someone to Carry

I'm glad we're moving into the holiday season, because the kids need something to celebrate. Last night they about brought down the roof just because Patrick tried to take a first step. His cheering section turned rowdy when his face hit the floor. You'd think they'd never seen a baby bite the dust before. How short their memories.

As I watch Patrick fumble around the furniture, feeling his way and pondering the finer points of putting his best foot forward, I realize we're heading toward another family reunion this week. The crash clan is scheduled to take Great-grandmother's house by storm for Thanksgiving. We do this every year, except when a baby is due. After we leave, the rest of the family knows what to get Great Nanny and Papa for Christmas: They replace the things the Hunter boys broke.

It's startling to think how clearly I can remember four other Hunter kids going to their grandmother's for Thanksgiving. It may have been two girls and two boys, but they were just as disruptive as the four I'm trying to tame by Turkey Day. Could it have really been a couple of decades ago? All the same faces show up, but there are a lot of new ones, tiny ones, optimistic and cheerful ones who can tear apart a turkey or a table in seconds flat—whatever is called for.

Pity poor Patrick. His timing is off. If he had ever been to a family reunion before, he would know that he should be walking before now. He had the rotten luck to be born about this time last year. That means he will turn one year old about two weeks after Thanksgiving. Pitiful timing. No one wants to have a birthday close to Christmas, and no one wants to have to take his first steps *after* the family has psychoanalyzed his feet.

First, he'll have to endure the stories of how all his cousins were walking at eleven months and jogging with their daddies by their first birthday. If he sits on the floor with a couple of blocks and doesn't stack them in two seconds flat, aunts will exchange worried glances. "He's a little slow, isn't he?" they'll ask. "He'll grow out of it—probably," they'll console.

Now if Patrick was our first, we could make up all those glorious first-baby stories about how he does handstands at home but refuses to perform before the public. We could plead with him to recite his ABC's and then admit that he usually gets R and S reversed anyway, so it's probably good he's not in the mood to show off. Then we could tell them he's probably just a little off today because he's made up his mind to be potty trained by his first birthday and he's realizing he has only two weeks left.

Amazing isn't it, how much more honest parents get with their third or fourth child? With Zachary, six years ago, I took the role of full-time coach and coaxed and pleaded with his tiny legs to support his chunky body and take at least one baby step on his first birthday. It worked. At his first birthday party, he took two steps, fell flat on his face on a hard floor, busted his lip, bit his tongue, and bloodied his birthday suit. We recorded the whole event on film, and I swore off coaching. I didn't involve myself at all, for instance, in the diaper wars that came with potty training.

I like having a crawler, because it makes me feel a little bit younger. Every time we put away the last box of diapers and the baby looks like he lost twenty pounds around the middle, I realize how much I've gained around the middle. Watching children grow has a peculiarly torturous aspect.

I used to complain about always having to carry somebody—some little body. I don't complain anymore. I can see just a little bit down the road, to where no one wants to be carried anymore. They're all walking—sometimes beside me, sometimes way out front, sometimes with me, and sometimes away from me. The times they need to be carried will be all too infrequent. Too many times my need to carry will remain unmet. So, Patrick, take your time. Keep falling a little longer, so I can pick you up.

49 You Take Ballet. I Get the Boys

It was either the ballet or the boys; *The Nutcracker* or the house wreckers. I could either watch toys dance on the stage or fly through the air. The choice was mine, and I opted for "mine." I stayed home with the boys while Mom went to the ballet with a friend, something ladies can do but men cannot.

We passed each other at the front door long enough for her to tell me two of the boys were a shade under the weather, one of them was having a friend over for dinner, there was nothing to eat, and the refrigerator was making funny sounds again. "Have a good evening," she said. "You watch your sugarplums and I'll watch mine."

Things could have looked bleak if I hadn't had advance warning so I could arrive with frozen pizzas and *Mary Poppins.* (All right, so Mary Poppins is not exactly macho. They go for anything that can fly—even with an umbrella.)

Dinner was no problem. We made a pact to break all the harmless rules. They got to eat in the living room—a no-no. They got all the dessert they wanted. They got to jump off the couch into the beanbags. They got to do almost anything they wanted to do, as long as they left me alone. You see, I had something to prove.

It was that trace of a snicker on Lisa's face, that implication of incompetence with which she said good-bye. I knew that she just knew she'd come home to a wrecked house, dirty dishes, kids with faces so sticky they were stuck to their pillows, and a Dad sitting in a corner hugging a stuffed E.T., blubbering something about better birth control.

She would have sighed, sat her purse down on the coffee table, turned slowly around the living room on her high heels in her best ballet imitation of grace, and said something like, "Well, well. Did we have a good evening with the boys?" I could just envision her beginning the next day with her hair tied back—boiling the sheets, moving the furniture out to air in the sun, stripping the floors. She would delight in restoring our home to its predisaster days. Lysol stock would triple by Monday on the New York Stock Exchange. She would have proven again, "There's no place like home if there's no one like Mom."

While they watched TV, I did laundry. While they demolished the downstairs, I cleaned the upstairs. After they were totally exhausted, I sent them upstairs. I made sure they were too weak to wreck. I unloaded the dishes *she* had left, washed another load, and put them away. I destroyed the pizza boxes, so she wouldn't know we hadn't had something harder to fix. I baked eight dozen cookies. (I meant to bake four dozen, but accidentally doubled one ingredient—the water. This necessitated doubling everything else.)

"If your mother asks you tomorrow morning, you tell her you had a bath," I told them as I tucked them in.

"But that's a lie," one replied.

"Then just ignore her," I said.

I put away everything I could find the proper place for and pitched the rest in the hall closet. I turned the shower on briefly, so the bathtub would be wet. I arranged a few dried flowers and put them with the cookies on the bar. Quickly I ran to the nursery to hide two disposable diapers, so she wouldn't realize I had changed the baby only once all evening.

About this time I heard that most dreaded of nighttime noises: the sound of an upchucking child.

"Keep it in. I'm coming," I yelled as I raced up the stairs, grabbed Donovan, and ran to the toilet. We made it. The poor kid was so afraid to throw up, I think I cured him.

When Lisa got home, I was reclining in the easy chair, eating cookies in a sparkling clean house, realizing I cheated myself out of my end of the bargain. She got her ballet, but I missed the boys altogether.

Like I've told her before, a *home* can be so clean, it just becomes a house.

50 Somewhere Someone's Leaving Someone

Somewhere someone's leaving someone, right this very minute: slamming a door, packing a suitcase, writing a note, kissing a forehead, trading a future for memories, leaving tears on tiny cheeks and questions in little minds, but leaving.

It happens a lot in the world of the seven-year-old, just like learning to read and wrestle by the rules. Just when you think you're no longer afraid of the dark, it becomes a little blacker and more threatening. Just when you thought you'd found a source with all the answers, you're left with all your questions.

I know a seven-year-old who spends lots of time parading in his security. You know, that cocky way a child behaves when he knows the world was created only for his pleasure? Every sentence begins with "Look at me," because he believes the people around him are interested only in what he's doing. He talks all the time, partly because he assumes we're always listening. He falls asleep easily and wakes up excited. His room is cluttered, but his mind is clear.

Actually, he's not seven yet, but still a month shy. I just thought it would be a good time to tell him that seven will be just another birthday and not a new beginning; not an ending, either. He's going to be stuck with the same old parents.

You see, I knew another seven-year-old once. He was just as childishly pompous about his world. He was expanding his horizons and had recently taken up crawdad fishing with his dad. He kept sneaking bacon from the fridge and making his way down to the creek across the railroad tracks, tying it to strings, and trying to catch a bigger crawdad than his daddy could. Still, somehow his daddy always found the bigger one. Just like the time they went frog gigging and the boy came up empty while the daddy was able to get enough frog legs to fill the family later that night.

Well, that was twenty-three years ago, and a lot of water has flowed through the creek where the crawdads scampered into the pond where the frogs jumped and croaked. And now the seven-year-old has a seven-year-old of his own.

I wonder what the people who once loved each other say

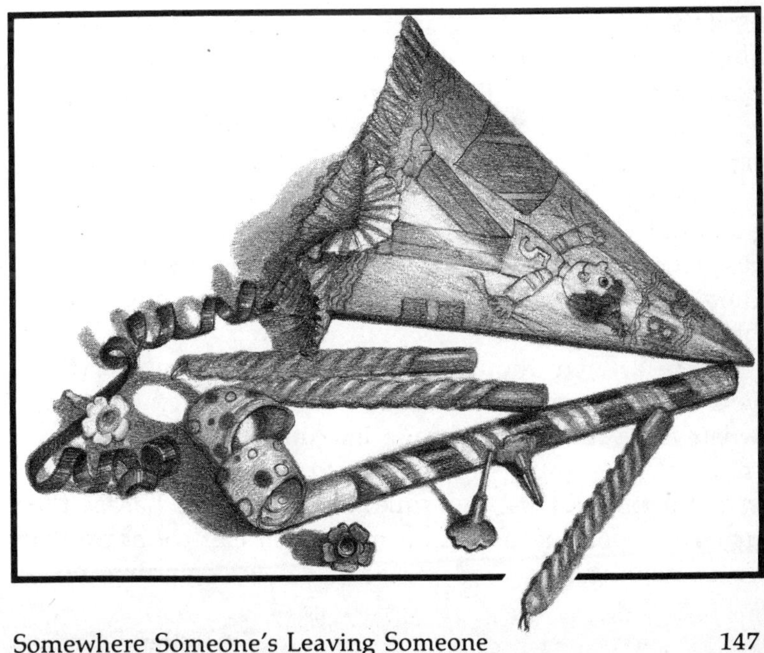

to each other when they plan never to see each other again? "I couldn't live without you once, but now I can." "Please don't take this personally." "I'm not good enough for you, but for someone else I'm okay." "Take care." "Take care, heck. I'm taking *everything.*"

I really don't know what a union says to itself when it dissolves. I've never been privy to the private conversations that precede one becoming two again. I used to wonder what my daddy must have said to my mother the last time they talked in person. As children, we are spared that and left to wonder. It is a wondering that leads to dreams that the one who left will come back, that a terrible mistake was made and will be corrected, that we'll all wake up and take another family vacation.

Even worse than the wondering about what they said to each other is the reality of what they say to the child. "It will be all right; you'll see." Even by the time we're seven, we've been clued to know that "It's all right; you'll see" from a grown-up comes only when the tragedy is final. It's way past "We'll work it out," or "Sleep tight, dream the night, in the morning it'll be all right." When a parent fakes a smile, squeezes you unfamiliarly hard, looks you directly in the eye, and says, "You'll see," every bone in your body screams silently, "I will not!"

And it isn't true that time heals all wounds. Like a tiny splinter left unremoved, the worst events of childhood, like divorce, can lay unnoticed until something brushes against them and stirs a little prick of pain. Like a son's seventh birthday.

And so, Zach, though I likely won't get you everything you want for your birthday, I promise not to take away whatever security you parade in. And while turning seven may not have much significance to you, to me it's a giant step for both of us. If I squeeze you a little harder than usual, it's not because I'm leaving. You can count on that, year after year.

51 Sadness at the Sound of Trains

Somebody asked me the other day about the name for this book. They wanted to know if I really want my sons to be like me when they grow up. I'll never tell. Actually, there are times when I wouldn't wish me on anyone. Then, like anyone else, I have the right to think I'm pretty much okay at other times.

Someone a little more personal said something like, "I bet you were really close to your dad, and that's why you like being a father so much, huh?" I wish that were true, for one of my deepest beliefs is that a son needs his father. Another of my deepest beliefs is that many of the current ills in society can be traced to "daddyless children"—those who have fathers, but not father figures.

Once there was a little boy about seven who spent a lot of time in tree houses and playing with a white dog under a sycamore tree on Texas Street. He would lie on his back and hold his breath, daring butterflies to land on his nose, and pull blades of grass from the ground with his bare toes. In the evening he would wander to the railroad tracks around sunset and listen for the train and count the boxcars, imagining grizzled hoboes in each, escaping to a life of ease. Back at home, the bathwater would turn a dirty gray and sand would settle on the bottom, but he would emerge pink and healthy, ready to dream into another day.

And then one day he sat beneath his tree with no energy to climb and held his dog closely, rather than romping in the deep grass. In his anger, he could have swatted the butterflies he normally befriended. At sunset the sound of the approaching train seemed sadder than ever, its plaintive wail not crying of freedom, but only of despair. In the darkness of his room he didn't dream, for he found it hard to sleep. His daddy had gone.

Mixed with his loneliness were real fears. Taught from birth that Daddy would always protect him, he had believed it. Told over and over that "someday" I'll teach you "how to do this or that," he had always looked forward to "someday." Told over and over again how special he was, he had believed it. Now he felt left behind and very unspecial. How many times he had told his friends about his daddy, and they told him about theirs. Everyone was going to grow up to be like his daddy—that was what being little was all about in those days.

As he grew up, he saw his daddy now and then, but less and less often as the years went by. He always tried to retain the memories and would sit with his sister and recall with her the good times. Even when he was grown, he still called the man Daddy, because he hadn't been allowed the transition to Father or Dad or Pops or whatever older sons called older daddies.

In a society where the emphasis is on making things disposable, I think some people became convinced that parents weren't all that necessary. Perhaps it was thought that play and learning and encouragement from a grown-up, along with green beans and lots of sunshine, would grow healthy, happy children and eventually normal, productive adults. Throw in a few weekend visits and your child could be a real achiever. He would have learned about the "realities of life" at an early age. Psychologists decided that kids were tough and very resilient and adaptable. Divorce became justified more than ever, and worry over the children lessened as "experts" produced studies showing that children of one-parent homes didn't necessarily have a handicap. We may look back some day at the 1970s and recall the dumbness of society with revulsion.

In the meantime, many of those well-adjusted children played, learned, grew healthy eating their green beans and soaking up their sunshine, and then crawled off occasionally into corners and cried, asking themselves questions they wouldn't have had, if their parents had been around to answer them.

Someone will think I wrote this to point a finger at people who divorce. That's not true. I'm answering the question about fathers and sons. No, I wasn't close to my father, because he wasn't there. I never got good at building tree houses. My dog, Whitey, ran away, and I still get sad at the sound of trains. As for my sons, I want them to have the choice of being like me—to know me well enough to decide for themselves.

One thing I do remember: My dad wanted to be a writer.

52 A Porch for the Dreamers

When I was a kid, about ten, most houses had big porches across the front which, on a moment's notice, could be converted to battleships, castles, mountains, airplanes, stages, and bull rings. I died a thousand deaths, captivated a million audiences, saved a hundred nations, and conquered foe after foe, never in vain.

I don't remember being bored at that age, though I didn't have a computer (neither did anyone else), a video cassette recorder (neither did anyone else), or a motorcycle (I admit it: it seemed like everyone else had one).

Times change.

As a family, we're still in spring. Our children are like little buds. They're just newly planted and expend their energy reaching for the light, always expecting it to shine, always surprised at the clouds and rain, shocked at the thunder, and perturbed at the cold and dark. We still have to do most of the important things for them. Some of them can get legs in jeans, but haven't conquered zippers and snaps. Others barely know what pants are.

I'm anxious for the summertime of family life, when they toughen and test the climate, sending their roots out for cooler waters, bracing for the occasional storm, learning to take the heat that comes from standing in the sun. By this time, I hope they'll be well grounded and able, and we can sometimes sit in their shade as they do a few things for us.

And then will come the fall, when cool breezes will come in the form of silences of disagreement perhaps, or misunderstandings about the course of the future. In the fall of family life, each member sheds his cover and becomes who he truly is, like a tree bares its limbs and shows its true strength before the bitter winds and cruel snows. If they can bend and not break, we know their roots are firmly planted.

At the age of thirty-two, it is nearly impossible to imagine a winter in our family life, where we may call on our boys to care for us almost as much as we care for them today, to meet our needs, to love and listen, to share that season like we shared our springtime with them when we had the strength.

I know it's hard to imagine, especially when the baby still wakes us up at night. Still, if I close my eyes, I can imagine my grandfather at ten, barefoot in overalls, standing on a huge front porch of a dusty frame house—commanding a battleship or captivating an audience, but never thinking about a winter that would someday come, with leaves piled in the yard and snow drifting on the porches where the dreamers take the stage.

Epilogue
Not Just a Passing Fantasy

Lo and behold . . . some babies do *wear pink.*

Dear Lauren,

Where does the time go? It seems like only yesterday you were born, but it's already been four whole days of wonder-filled hours. I spent them convincing myself that you were indeed not just a passing fantasy, after all. And I discovered this: I really did want a baby daughter, and sometimes we do get what we want. Today, I overflow with fulfillment.

I got home last night after you went to sleep. I left this morning before you awoke, and in my tiredness of the night, I slept through all your feedings and changings. When I rushed out this morning to write these words, I stopped beside your bed to measure you with my eyes. I bent low to hear you breathe, and your puckered lips made a soft wet noise, like a kiss. So I kissed you.

On the way to work, I watched the birds flit back and forth across the highway and thought to myself, "Lauren doesn't know what a bird is," and I wanted to tell you all about them. What a beautiful world awaits you, beautiful one.

And wait it has, as we all have. God took His time sending you to us. He waited until He had created a place so full of love and protection that when He placed you here with four big brothers to watch over you, He surveyed the joy, like He likes to do, and surely said, "It is good."

Forgive me, Lauren, but even after we dressed you in the little pink dress I ran to get at the store, you looked suspiciously like Zachary with your fat cheeks, Russell with your pronounced chin, Donovan with your full, round eyes, and Patrick with your soft, dark hair. Forgive me, but I guess you looked like just another son with a dress and bows.

But you're not. You will have a quiet little voice, sparkling blue eyes, long, soft hair in curls, tiny feet, small and dainty toenails, eyelashes that flutter on tender cheeks when you laugh, and a dainty chin that will shyly quiver when you cry.

Lauren, while it's true that birds are beautiful and so is much of the world, it is not always beautiful. I wish I could make it that way for you; that you could sit and play with toys and listen to stories and grow with a painless heart and body, but it isn't always so. Today *is* full of joy, but not all days are.

So when someone breaks your heart and you feel like you want to die, I'll sit with you and hold you and tell you about the day you came to life for me, and the powerful and permanent joy we share may be able to keep us both going until your heart mends. And when your heart mends, mine will, too.

I used to think it was just the idle passing of time to dream of a little girl climbing into my lap, falling asleep, breathing softly against my neck. I thought it was futile to think of slumber parties, baby dolls, and the smell of permanents wafting from the dining room. Fun futility, I thought. But there *you* are, threatening my security with your mysterious presence.

But when I touched you, the very moment you first breathed in and returned your first audible cry, life changed again for me. I became a privileged man, with an opportunity to witness the beginning of a life that will be filled with giving and loving and sacrifice and beauty and joy as a baby becomes an awkward little girl, an obnoxious teenager, a beautiful young woman, a lovely lady, and a mother. Your first cry brought shivers for all it portends.

When I get home today, I'll hold you a little, then put you down and find my sons—your brothers. How lucky we all are to have one another to love. And I'll spend the evening making memories, which we all depend on for the rest of our lives. For memories can mend when life tears and breaks us. Memories can reweave a tatter in the fabric of our family. Memories can restore us when we fall, heal us when we hurt.

And I'll always remember the day my fantasy became real.

Welcome home, Lauren Alissa.

And another story begins.